LOOM BEADING
Patterns & Techniques

Ann Benson

Ann Benson Publishing
annbensonbeading.com
Port Orange, Florida
South Dennis, Massachusetts

ISBN 978-0-9996230-2-2

For Aunt Sally with love

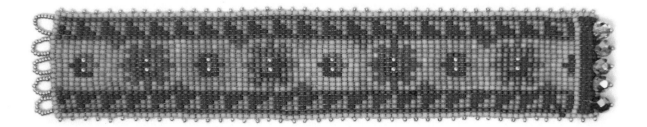

The focus of this work is loom beading,

more specifically, loom-beaded jewelry. The design patterns are for the most part long and narrow, and all of the loomed examples are either bracelets or necklaces. That said, you can use these patterns for anything that can be decorated with a strip of woven beads—the face of a small clutch, a phone purse, your guitar strap, napkin rings, the front of your motorcycle helmet. Use your imagination!

Loom weaving is a long-established craft with a wealth of available tutorial information in both print and digital format. I encourage you to go beyond the very basic techniques on these pages and experiment with both looms and materials. At the end of this book you'll find information about links to digital and print information in support of that journey.

My very first piece of beading at age eight was a woven ring, fashioned with seed beads from a local five-and-dime store. I wove it in hand with fine wire, but it wasn't long before I had a little loom, and the rest is history.

Bead on! You're making the world a better place.

Ann Benson

Contents

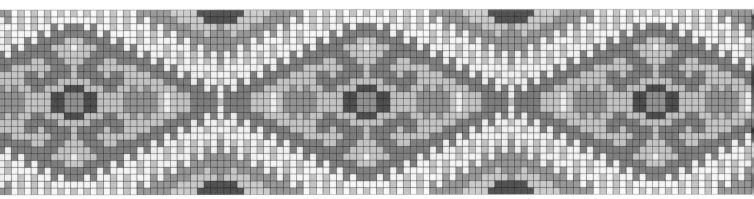

The basics of bead looming

The loom is warped. The weaving (weft) thread is attached. The w8eaving thread is loaded with beads in pattern. The threaded beads are positioned under the warp, pushed upward through the warp. The weaving thread is passed through the beads over the warp threads. Details, as they say, to follow.

Warp the loom based on the size of your project, following the directions of the loom's manufacturer. You'll need one warp for each bead in the width PLUS ONE.

In a nine-bead width you'll need ten warp threads

Secure the weft thread on the outside warp with a simple knot. If you're right handed, secure the thread on the left. If left handed, secure the thread on the right.

Pick up the beads of the first row. Run the thread UNDER the warps and press the beads upward between the warp threads with your fingertips across the row.

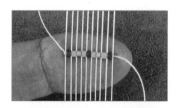

Secure the weft thread on the outer warp opposite of your dominant hand

Run the needle back through the beads of the first row, OVER the warp thread. It's very important to avoid piercing the warp threads with your needle. You may need to move the weave on the warps, and if the weft has been run through the warp thread, you will not be able to move the weave.

Take the slack out of the thread so there is little or no space between the warp threads and the beads. Don't pull so tightly that the width puckers; the width should be as consistent as possible from the start to the end of the weave. This completes the first row.

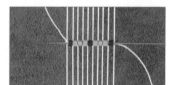

Press the beads upward between the beads with your fingertips

As you continue weaving, loop the thread from the front of the weave to the underside of the weave on each row. Continue adding rows, following your design chart or text, until you run out of thread. Leave at least a 3" (8cm) thread tail intact so you can secure it later.

Run the thread back through the beads OVER the warp, without piercing the warp thread

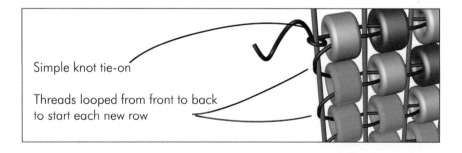

Simple knot tie-on

Threads looped from front to back to start each new row

The slack is taken out of the weft and the beads sit neatly between the warps

Secure the new thread in the same manner as for the first row. Continue weaving rows according to your design chart until you need a new thread again. Work in this manner until the predetermined length, taking into consideration the finishing method you've chosen.

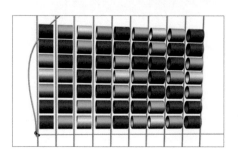

Uh oh. The weft thread pierces the warp. Note that as the rest of the row is moved, the piercing point is rigid and will not move. Press upward with your fingertip as you weave the weft through the beads; you may also find that a finer needle is helpful. Move each row before going on to the next to be sure you have not pierced.

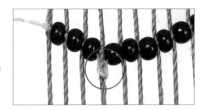

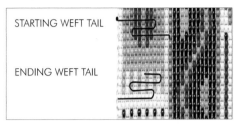

STARTING WEFT TAIL

ENDING WEFT TAIL

Secure the weft thread ends. The starting tail should be secured in the rows AFTER the attachment point, and the end tails should be secured in the rows BEFORE the ending point. Note that if you don't mind weaving with thread ends unsecured, those ends can later be used for finishing and decoration when the weave is complete.

About seed beads

These are the most popular seed beads for bead looming. You can experiment with other shapes and sizes such as cubes, triangles, and multi-hole beads. You'll adapt your warp spacing to fit the bead size. Miyuki Delica numbers are used herein; you can substitute other styles by matching to the color bar included in each design page. When choosing colors, opaque and opaque matte colors are the best choice. The obvious exception to this is decorative or metallic beads. The most important factor in making design elements pop is CONTRAST. Avoid combining colors that are close in value.

 Japanese 15°s (1.3 x 1.5 mm) Miyuki and Toho are the same size, Matsunos tend to be a bit larger. Intricate patterns can be created with this size bead. Use a finer thread such as Nymo B or C-Lon AA as thread buildup can be a problem. Size 12 needles can work, but have a size 13 on hand.

 Japanese cylinder beads (1.6 x 1.5 mm) (Delicas, Aikos/Treasures). Size 11 is standard, but they are also available in size 15 (1.3 x 1 mm) and larger sizes. The weave will have squared edges and a precise, clean appearance. With large holes they're a dream to weave. There is a huge color range, readily available.

 Czech 11°s (2 x 1 mm) are more elliptical in shape than Japanese, so weaves made entirely from this type of bead will have great flexibility. Amazing color range, very good availability.

 Japanese 11°s (2.1 x 1.1 mm) have larger holes than Czech and their edges are generally more squared. Weaves made entirely from Japanese 11°s are very neat and consistent in appearance. Thousands of colors, great availability. Czech 10°s are fairly close in size to Japanese 11°s.

 Czech 8°s (3 x 2 mm) and Japanese 8°s (3.1 x 2.1 mm) have good-sized holes. They have weight and substance. As with 11°s, Czech 8°s tend to be slightly more rounded than Japanese.

 Japanese and Czech 6° (4 x 3 mm) seed beads are quite varied in size within brands and all are heavy, so they are a bit difficult to weave, but they make great embellishments when worked together with other sizes of beads.

Weaving needles

Size 12 needles are the ones you will use most for weaving; the long looming needle is great for wider pieces, the regular beading needle for narrower pieces. The embroidery needle has a stronger shaft and will come in handy for close work and weaving in thread ends. Size 9 darning needles will be a good choice for any fiber work you may add, and the size 13 beading needle comes in handy when you have small beads or thread build-up.

Size 12 long beading looming needle

Size 12 regular beading needle

Size 13 beading needle

Size 9 darning needle

Size 12 embroidery needle

Choosing a loom

A small loom (less than 12" length) will suffice for almost all of them unless you are repeating patterns to achieve greater length. You may already own a loom that you adore and you can do any of these pieces using a standard loom.

There are two types of looms used for jewelry: those that require finishing of the end warp threads (traditional looms) and those that require no or minimal finishing (no-finish looms). This type was used to create all the pieces herein and has the advantage of ease in finishing, but has limits in sizing. You'll need to "cram" in rows of beads so that when the work is removed from the loom, the end thread loops can be hidden within the weave by decompressing the weave.

Traditional looms have the advantage of open sizing so you can size on-the-fly; when the weave is the right length, you just stop weaving and then weave the end threads into the work prior to adding closures. Some traditional loom brands such as Mirrix have adapters available for no-finish weaving. Any loom you use should allow a "sett" (essentially, warps per inch) of between 10 and 20 for beads sized 8° to 15°. You can double up threads and then separate them while weaving if your loom has a wider sett, but most jewelry looms will accommodate bead sizes easily.

My No-Finish loom can be warped up to 8.5" long; it's lightweight and portable. The loom can be disassembled with the work intact in progress for easy travel.

About threads

The threads that run between the beads are called warp. The carrying thread that holds the beads is called "weft." Sometimes the same thread can be used for both warp and weaving, especially with smaller sizes of beads. Sometimes you will need two very different threads. Regardless, the threads used for any project must have some very specific qualities:

STRENGTH Warp thread needs to have enough strength to withstand the tension of being stretched taut on the loom. Weaving threads need to be resistant to friction from the inside of the beads, which are not always smooth. Waxing and conditioning thread can improve its strength.

STABILITY Warp thread especially should not be stretchy. It should maintain its integrity when pulled taut. The thread should not become longer when you yank it with some force.

DURABILITY You're putting a lot of time and effort into weaving your piece. THREAD IS MORTAL and natural fibers can degrade over the years, so some weavers avoid them entirely. Nylon, polyester, and cotton or silk blends are excellent choices. Soft fibers such as wook, tencel and rayon, while beautiful as fiber weft, will shrink when wet and will require reshaping similar to needlepoint blocking.

BLENDABILITY There are times when you want your warp thread to become part of the design itself (rag rugs are an example), and then you don't need to be concerned with this quality. But when working with small seed beads you will likely want your warp and weave thread to be less noticeable. Choose the lightest weight that's appropriate for your project, and choose a neutral color that blends into the overall color theme of the project. You will always be able to see threads at the edge of the weave, so keep it as invisible as possible.

Favorites for warping:
Conso nylon upholstery thread
C-Lon or S-Lon micro-cord
SoNo and Hana for smaller beads
Nymo nylon size D
Gutermann topstitching thread
Toho One-G nylon

For weaving (weft) threads
I almost exclusively use light to medium nylon beading thread, most often Nymo, S-Lon and C-Lon brands. For larger or heavier beads Toho One-G, SoNo and Hana are good choices.

Using the patterns

Most of the full patterns are shown on three or more pages; the first page will show the aspect ratio of the weave, the unit size of the design, the warp requirements, bead recommendations, and in some cases the inspiring graphics. Text patterns follow the graphic patterns, for those who prefer them. Review the information below for best use of the patterns.

EACH SQUARE/RECTANGLE ON THE CHART INDICATES ONE BEAD IN THE WEAVE

Each pattern is shown in two aspects: one for cylinder beads, and one for seed beads. Because these beads have different length and width ratios, the resulting woven size and appearance will be different. A design woven in seed beads will be narrower than the same design woven in cylinders. The page for that design will show the aspect differences in the full length of the pattern.

Design pages will give a chart indicating the width of the pattern in inches and centimeters based on the three most popular sizes of beads: size 11 cylinders, 15° seed beads, and 11° seed beads.

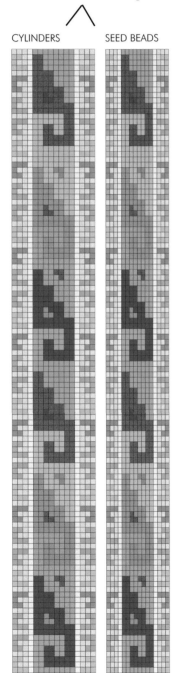

CYLINDERS   SEED BEADS

WIDTH/11-DELICAS	.95"	2.4Cm
WIDTH /15° SEED BEADS	.8"	2.1Cm
WIDTH /11° SEED BEADS	1"	2.5Cm

WARP THREADS REQUIRED 17
UNITS 16 X 125

Design pages show the number of warp threads required and the number of units shown in the pattern.

Delica 1591 (354)

Delica 2133 (152)

Delica 881 (236)

Delica 2112 (236)

Delica 352 (234)

Delica 1136 (258)

Delica 757 (158)

Delica 1597 (152)

Delica 758 (90)

Bead colors are given for Miyuki Delicas. Each design page shows a graphic color bar with the full range of colors for that design, the Miyuki Delica color number, and the number of beads required to weave the design as it is shown on the page (given in parentheses).Conversion charts are available on the internet for determining the corresponding color of seed beads and other brands of beads.

Where available, stitched or woven models of the pattern will be shown. Photos or graphics that inspired the pattern may also be shown.

Enlargements of the charted pattern are shown. In the case of mirrored and symmetrical patterns, the center point will be shown, along with specific directions for repeating the pattern to your length. When a pattern is continuous, the full length will be shown in pieces, with starting and continuation points shown. In repeating patterns, one repeat and the overall look will be shown along with a color bar.

MIRRORED OR SYMMETRICAL PATTERNS

▼ START

CENTER ROW

FULL LENGTH PATTERNS

▼ START

CONTINUE

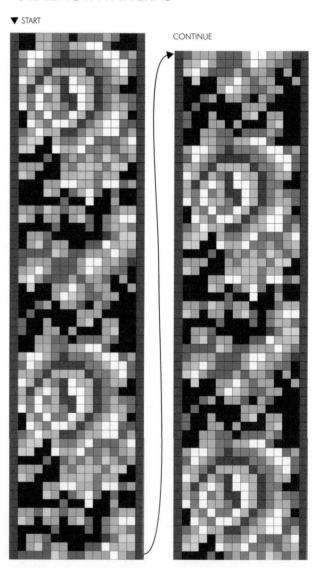

Sizing patterns for your desired result

If you're using a no-finish loom, you can set your warp length to the desired length. On a loom that requires end finishing, the warp should be longer than the desired length of the finished piece as you will need enough thread on each warp end to secure it within the weave. Your loom's directions for use will give recommendations on the matter of securing warp threads.

If your pattern is continuous, weave from one end to the other, of course taking into consideration the finishing method you'll use, discussed later.

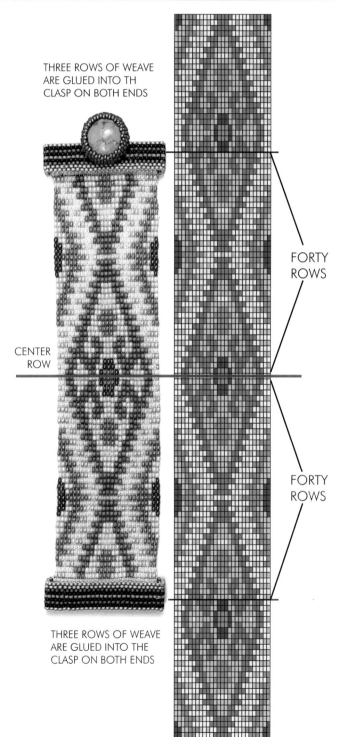

THREE ROWS OF WEAVE ARE GLUED INTO TH CLASP ON BOTH ENDS

FORTY ROWS

CENTER ROW

FORTY ROWS

THREE ROWS OF WEAVE ARE GLUED INTO THE CLASP ON BOTH ENDS

The number of woven rows per inch will differ between the various sizes of beads. These are lengths and widths for the most popular sizes:

Length:
Delicas (size 11) 15 rows per inch, 6 rows per centimeter
15° seed beads 16 rows per inch, 7 rows per centimeter
11° seed beads 12.5 rows per inch, 5 rows per centimeter

Width (including warp threads):
Delicas (size 11) 17Beads per inch, 7Beads per centimeter
15° seed beads 20Beads per inch, 8Beads per centimeter
11° seed beads 16 rows per inch, 6.5Beads per centimeter

If you're making a symmetrical weave, it's good practice to start at the center and weave outward. Set up your loom so the weavable length is what you want, then start weaving at the center and work outward. Theoretically you'll end up at the same point on both ends, or at least quite close.

In "Sierra" at right, the desired length of the weave is shown, taking into consideration the 1/4" that the clasp adds to the length. The finished length of this bracelet including the clasp is 6 3/4" (17.2Cm), which is a perfect fit for a 6.5" (16.5cm) wrist. The side-by-side photo and chart are just about the same size, and as you can see far less than the full chart is woven.

EXAMPLE: 6.5" of woven length is needed. 11° seed beads are used. There are 12.5 rows per inch of length with this size bead. Warp your loom so there are about 16 warps per inch.

6.5 x 12.5 = 81.5 rows. Round up or down to the nearest odd-numbered row, in this case 81. You need an odd number of rows because the center row is NOT repeated.

81 rows minus the center row = 80 rows
80 rows divided by 2 = 40 rows on each end outside the center row

Getting more out of the patterns

Patterns are shown in their full width, but many can be used in part, or with design added. For example, in "Delano" at right, three additional rows are added on both sides of the width, which maintains the general look of the design while adding more substance.

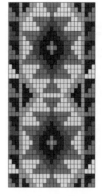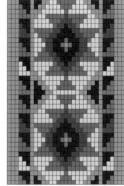

In this example, "December" has had three beads removed from both sides of the pattern; you can easily do this by taping paper over the elements you don't want to weave, so you won't have to be so vigilant about where you are starting and ending in each row.

"Delano" in original format and with three beads added on both sides

"December" in original format and with three rows removed on both sides

Use the straight edges of paper to cover over the areas you don't want to stitch

Making necklaces by doubling patterns

A pattern can be fully or partially doubled to form the two sides of a necklace, with a focal motif at the center base of the pattern as shown here. "Carol" is woven with a five-bead border on both sides as a bracelet; in the necklace the five-bead border is eliminated, resulting in a narrower weave. A weave that is more than 1.5" wide may not lay as nicely on the neck as a narrower one.

Strands of beads in graduating length are used to attach the focal motif to the woven strips. The length of these strands will vary depending on the shape of the motif.

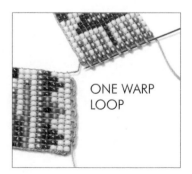

ONE WARP LOOP

If you have a no-finish loom, the end WITHOUT warp ends in a necklace should be at the center front, as the two sides will be joined by one warp loop when the weave is removed from the loom.

The Patterns   Page numbers shown on each image snippet

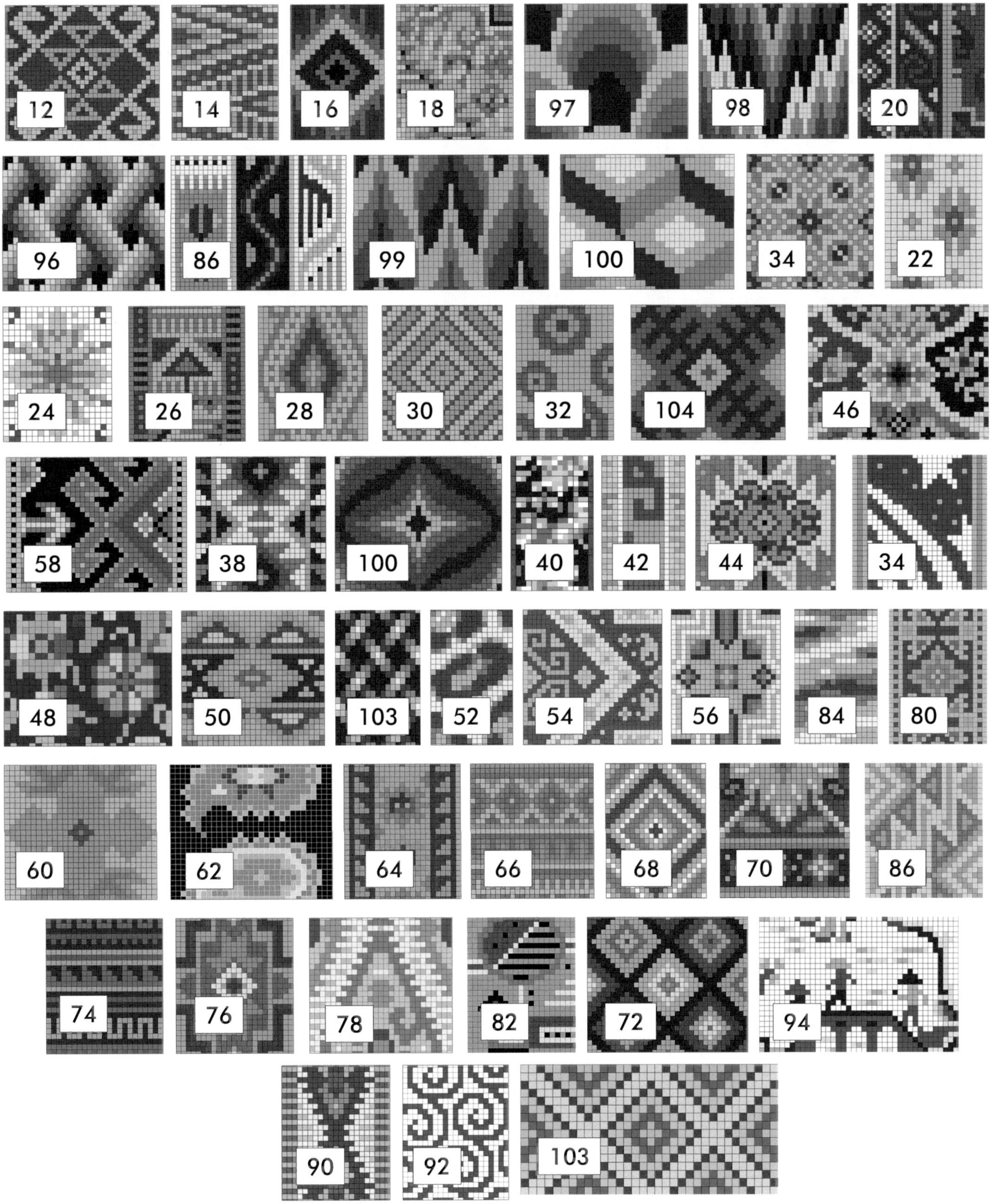

12 14 16 18 97 98 20

96 86 99 100 34 22

24 26 28 30 32 104 46

58 38 100 40 42 44 34

48 50 103 52 54 56 84 80

60 62 64 66 68 70 86

74 76 78 82 72 94

90 92 103

Alhambra

CYLINDERS   SEED BEADS

WIDTH/11-DELICAS	2"	5.2cm
WIDTH /15° SEED BEADS	1.75"	4.4cm
WIDTH /11° SEED BEADS	2.2"	5.6cm

WARP THREADS REQUIRED 36
UNITS 35 X 139

Delica 2288 (1608)

Delica 1581 (1288)

Delica 797 (1070)

Delica 374
 (902)

START

CENTER ROW

THIS ENLARGED CHART SHOWS HALF OF THIS REPEATING MOTIF DESIGN; TO COMPLETE THE DESIGN, REPEAT FROM THE START POINT TO THE DESIRED LENGTH. DO NOT REPEAT THE CENTER ROW (**OUTLINED IN RED**)

CYLINDERS

SEED BEADS

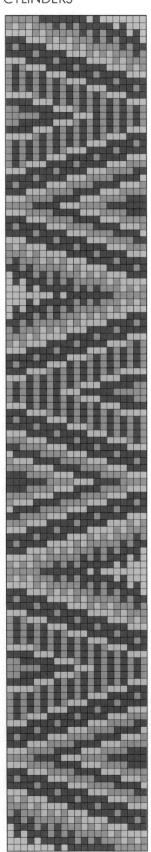

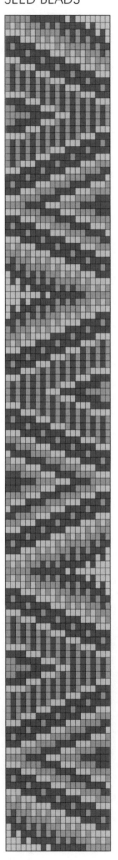

Arabesque

WIDTH/11-DELICAS	1.25"	3.1cm
WIDTH /15° SEED BEADS	1.1"	2.8cm
WIDTH /11° SEED BEADS	1.3"	3.3cm

WARP THREADS REQUIRED 22
UNITS 21 X 121

Delica 2359 (1091)

Delica 2309 (782)

Delica 1154 (668

Shown here in slightly
different colors of 12°
three-cut seed beads with
loop and bead closure.

START ▶

CONTINUE

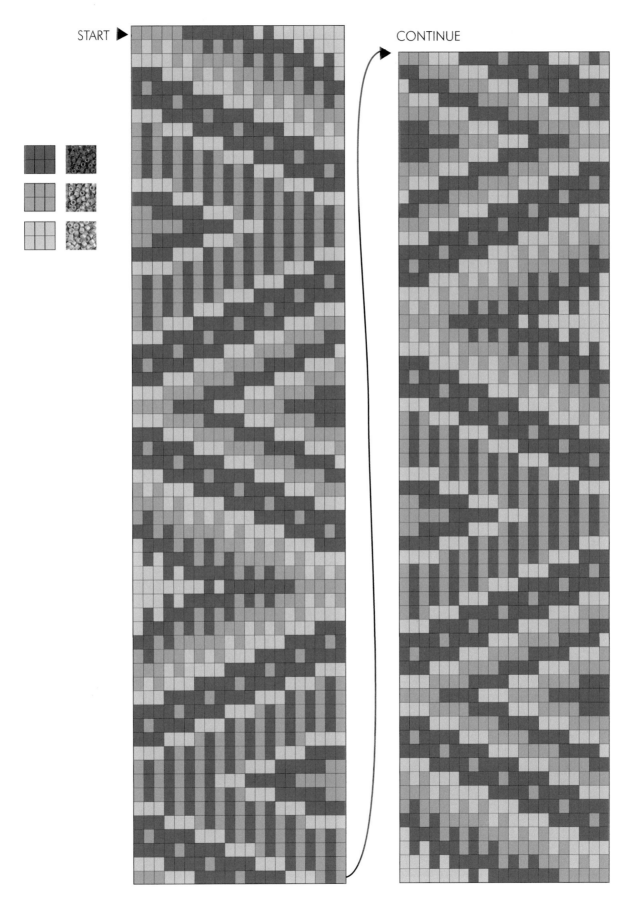

CYLINDERS   SEED BEADS

Arrows

WIDTH/11-DELICAS	1.1"	2.8cm
WIDTH /15° SEED BEADS	.95"	2.4cm
WIDTH /11° SEED BEADS	1.2"	3cm

WARP THREADS REQUIRED 20
UNITS 19 x 125

Delica 2140 (526)

Delica 2357 (422)

Delica 378 (388)

Delica 2286 (306)

Delica 723 (248)

Delica 2290 (248)

Delica 609 (207)

THIS ENLARGED CHART SHOWS HALF OF THE DESIGN; START AT THE CENTER POINT OF THE LOOM AND WORK OUTWARD FROM THE CENTER ROW (**OUTLINED IN RED**). ROTATE THE LOOM OR CHART AND WEAVE THE OTHER HALF OF THE DESIGN, **BUT DO NOT REPEAT THE CENTER ROW.**

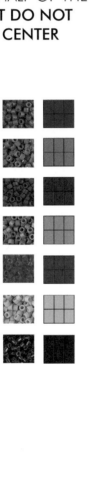

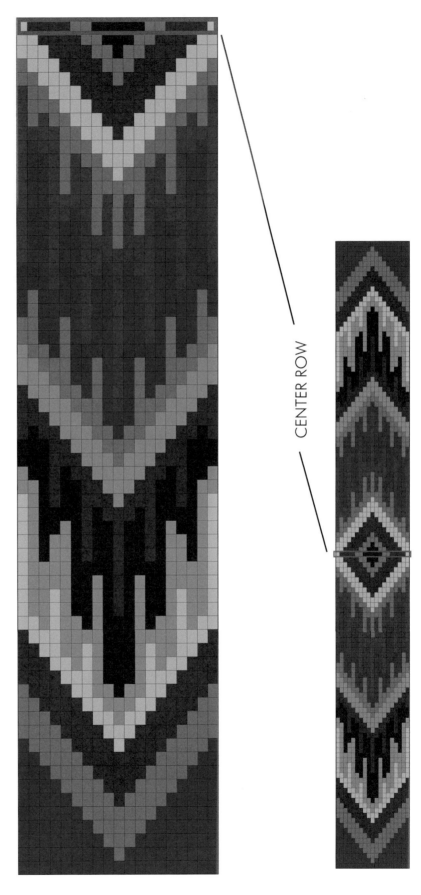

CENTER ROW

CYLINDERS

SEEDBEADS

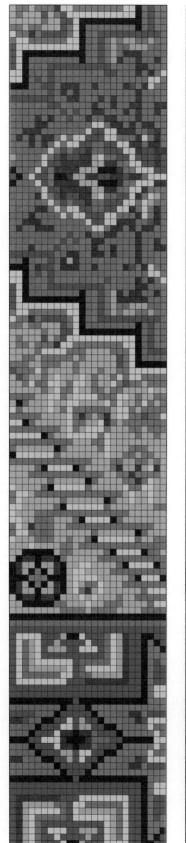

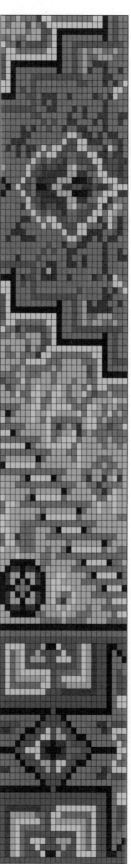

WIDTH/11-DELICAS	1.5"	3.7cm
WIDTH /15° SEEDBEADS	1.25"	3.2cm
WIDTH /11° SEEDBEADS	1.6"	4cm

WARP THREADS REQUIRED 26
UNITS 25 x 131

Delica 2143 (1617)

Delica 859 (755)

Delica 2309 (529)

Delica 2101 (290)

Delica 2125 (222)

Delica 2143 (57)

Delica 753 (67)

Delica 855 (XXX)

▼ START

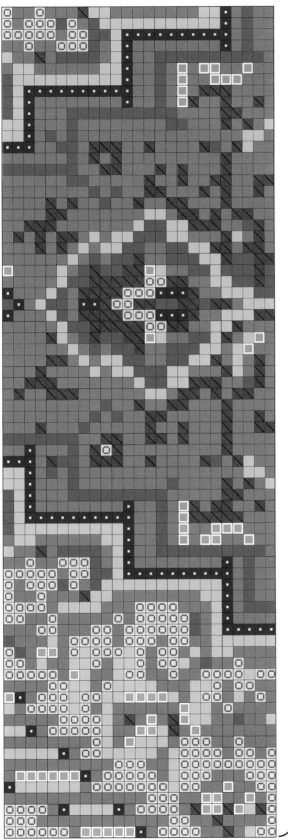

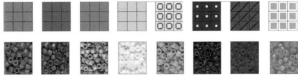

CONTINUE

CYLINDERS

SEED BEADS

WIDTH/11-DELICAS	1.6"	4.1 cm
WIDTH /15° SEED BEADS	1.35"	3.4 cm
WIDTH /11° SEED BEADS	1.7"	4.3 cm

WARP THREADS REQUIRED 28
UNITS 27 x 131

Delica 2143 (1617)

Delica 753 (755)

Delica 2309 (529)

Delica 2125 (290)

Delica 2110 (222)

Delica 797 (57)

Delica 2101 (67)

▼ START

CONTINUE

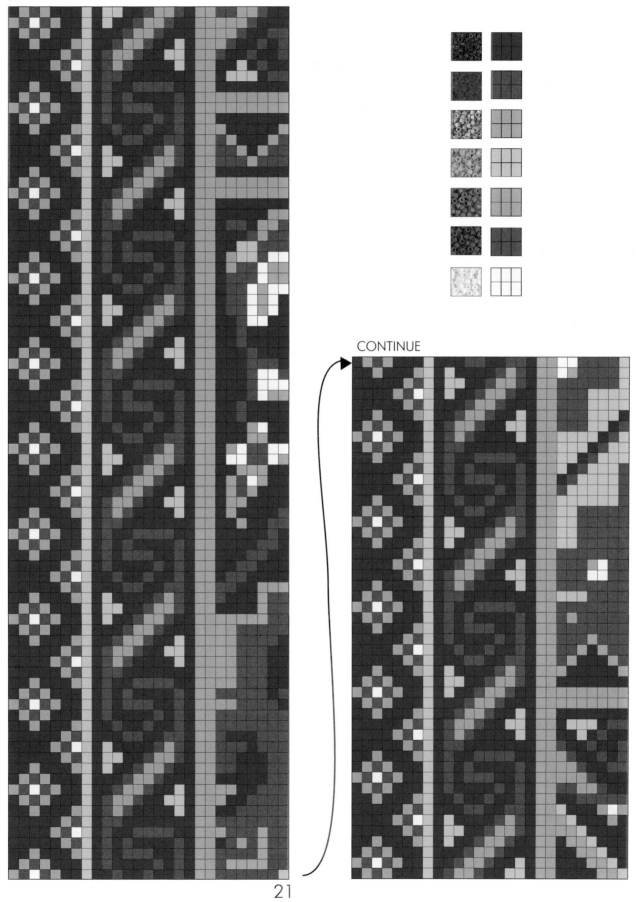

CYLINDERS   SEED BEADS

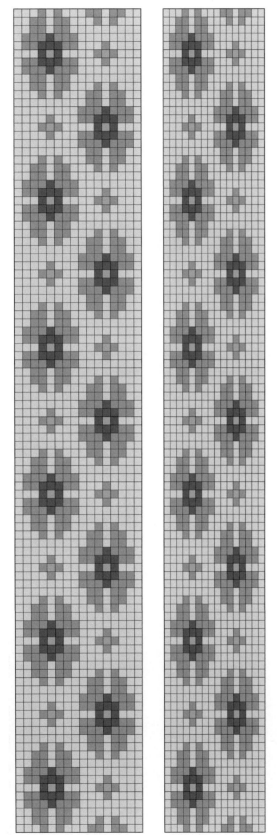

Brass Motifs

WIDTH/11-DELICAS	.95"	2.4 cm
WIDTH /15° SEED BEADS	.8"	2.1 cm
WIDTH /11° SEED BEADS	1"	2.5 cm

WARP THREADS REQUIRED 17
UNITS 16 X 101

Delica 2290 (988)

Delica 391 (496)

Delica 323 (110)

Delica 374 (22)

"Brass Motifs" tapestry bead crochet in
11° seed beads with a magnetic clasp

▼ START

CONTINUE

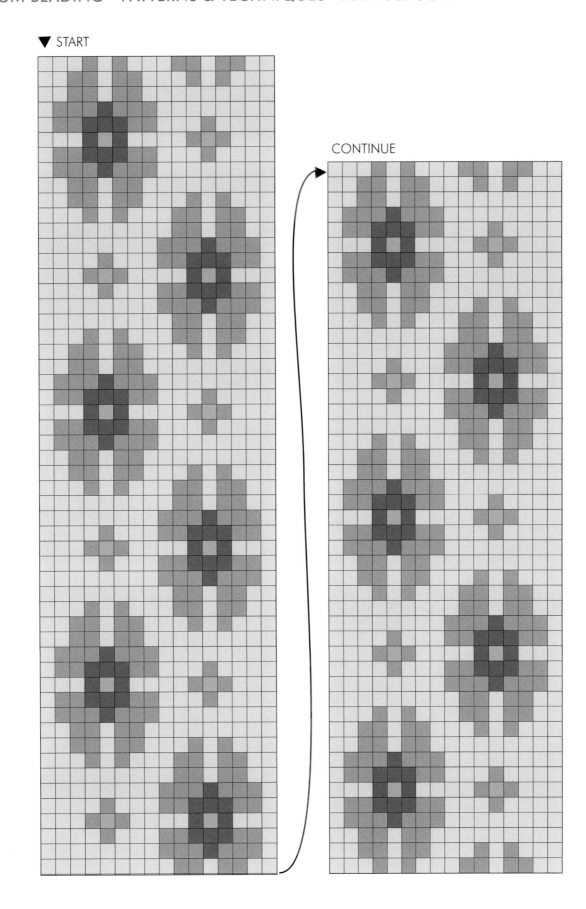

CYLINDERS   SEED BEADS

Caprice

WIDTH/11-DELICAS	1.13"	2.8 cm
WIDTH /15° SEED BEADS	,95"	2.4 cm
WIDTH /11° SEED BEADS	1.2"	3 cm

WARP THREADS REQUIRED 20
UNITS 19 x 107

Delica 351 (740)

Delica 872 (416)

Delica 881 (296)

Delica 2285 (160)

Delica 2136 (128)

Delica 2126 (116)

Delica 2140 (65)

Delica 656 (58)

Delica 2143 (54)

Caprice motifs used in a bead crochet purse

24

THIS ENLARGED CHART SHOWS HALF OF THE DESIGN; START AT THE CENTER POINT OF THE LOOM AND WORK OUTWARD FROM THE CENTER ROW **(OUTLINED IN RED)**. ROTATE THE LOOM OR CHART AND WEAVE THE OTHER HALF OF THE DESIGN, **BUT DO NOT REPEAT THE CENTER ROW.**

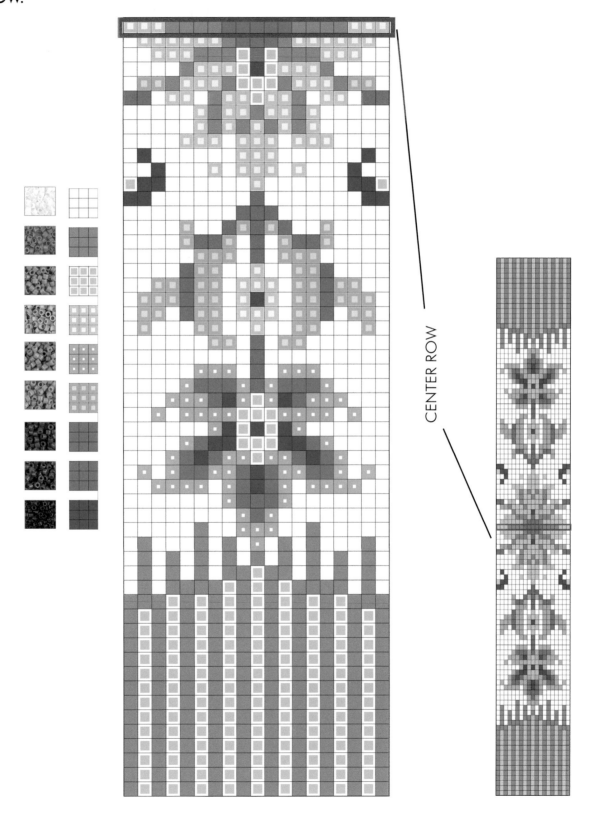

CENTER ROW

Carol

CYLINDERS   SEED BEADS

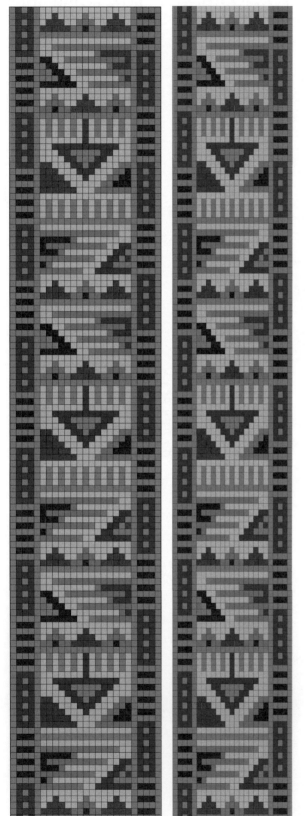

WIDTH/11-DELICAS	1.5"	3.7 cm
WIDTH /15° SEED BEADS	1.25"	3.2 cm
WIDTH /11° SEED BEADS	1.6"	4 cm

WARP THREADS REQUIRED 26
UNITS 25 X 131

 Delica 1153 1129)

 Delica 762 (858)

Delica 656 (528)

Delica 877 (352)

Delica 796 (274)

Delica 873 (132)

Shown here (smaller than actual size) for a 6" wrist in Japanese and Czech 11° seed beads, with buttonholes and pearls as the closure. The edging is a three-bead "picot" added after the weaving is complete.

▼ START

CONTINUE

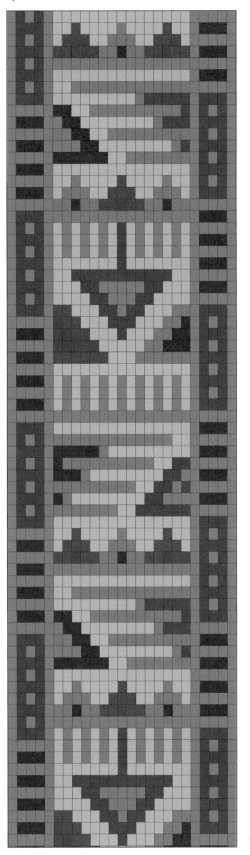

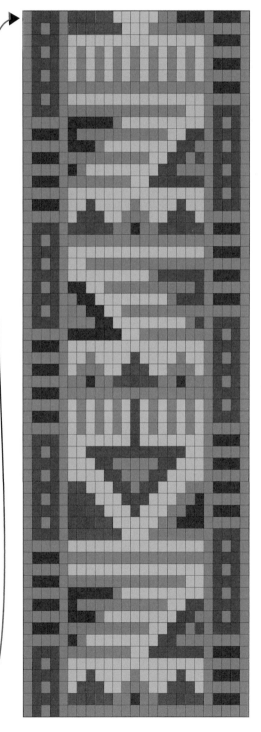

▼ START

CYLINDERS SEED BEADS

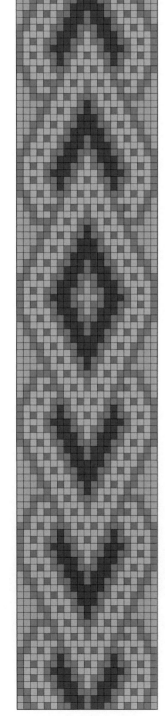

Chainstitch

WIDTH/11-DELICAS	1.25"	3.1cm
WIDTH /15° SEED BEADS	1.1"	2.8cm
WIDTH /11° SEED BEADS	1.3"	3.3cm

WARP THREADS REQUIRED 22
UNITS 21 X 119

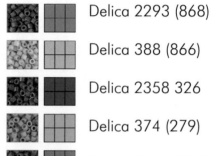

Delica 2293 (868)

Delica 388 (866)

Delica 2358 326

Delica 374 (279)

Delica 2118 (150)

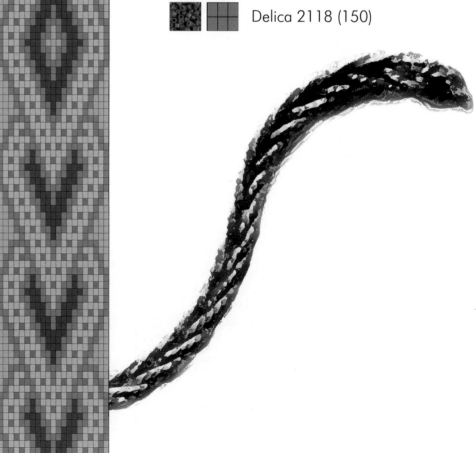

▼ START

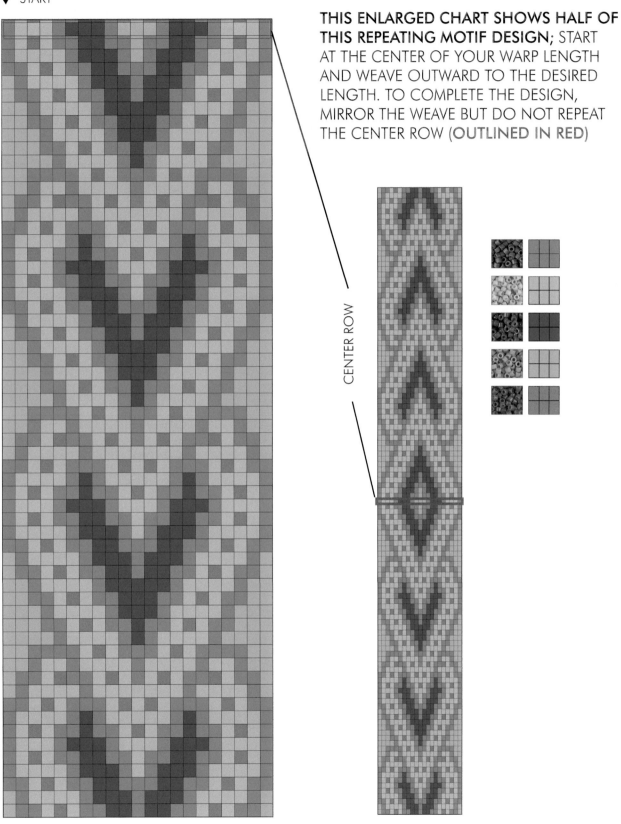

THIS ENLARGED CHART SHOWS HALF OF THIS REPEATING MOTIF DESIGN; START AT THE CENTER OF YOUR WARP LENGTH AND WEAVE OUTWARD TO THE DESIRED LENGTH. TO COMPLETE THE DESIGN, MIRROR THE WEAVE BUT DO NOT REPEAT THE CENTER ROW (**OUTLINED IN RED**)

CENTER ROW

CYLINDERS   SEED BEADS

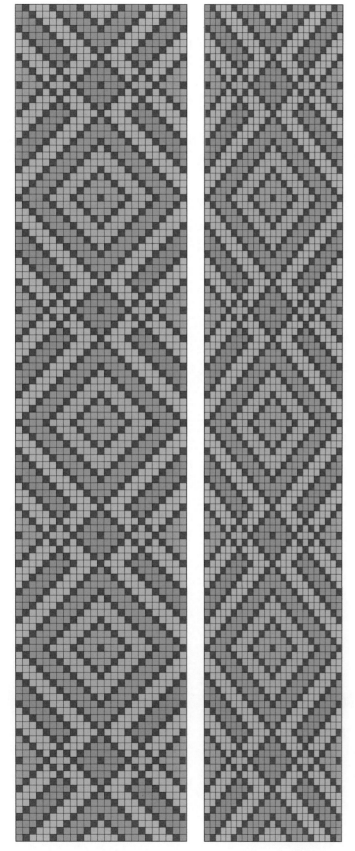

WIDTH/11-DELICAS	1.5"	3.7 cm
WIDTH /15° SEED BEADS	1.25"	3.2 cm
WIDTH /11° SEED BEADS	1.6"	4 cm

WARP THREADS REQUIRED 26
UNITS 25 x 119

Delica 729 (860)

Delica 340 (775)

Delica 760 (448)

Delica 800 (426)

Delica 2111 (274)

Delica 875 (201264)

START ▶

THIS ENLARGED CHART SHOWS HALF OF THIS MIRRORED DESIGN; START AT THE CENTER POINT OF THE LOOM AND WORK OUTWARD FROM THE CENTER ROW (OUTLINED IN RED).

CENTER ROW

CYLINDERS   SEED BEADS

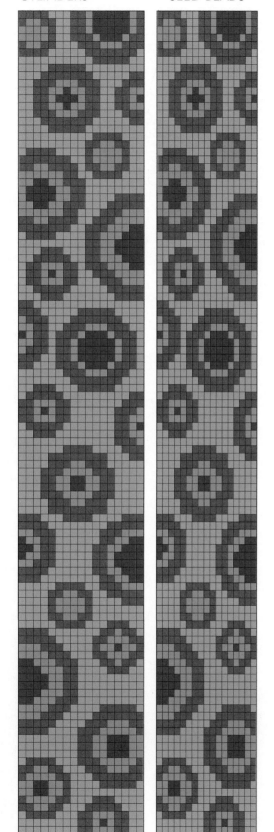

Circle Game

WIDTH/11-DELICAS	1"	2.5cm
WIDTH /15° SEED BEADS	.85"	2.2cm
WIDTH /11° SEED BEADS	1.1"	2.7cm

WARP THREADS REQUIRED 18
UNITS 17 X 108

Delica 356 (701)

Delica 753 (680)

Delica 2103 (317)

Delica 340 (138)

"Round Two" tapestry bead crochet
bracelet with copper magnetic clasp

▼ START

CONTINUE

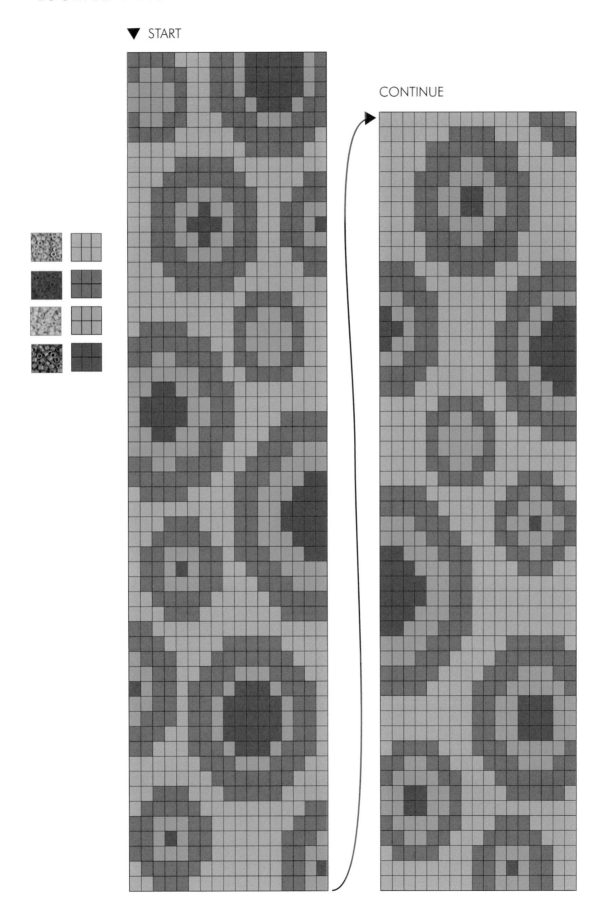

CYLINDERS

SEED BEADS

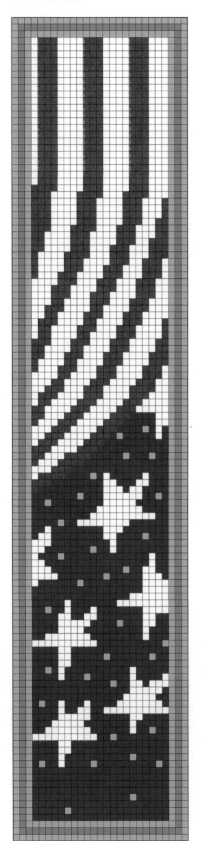

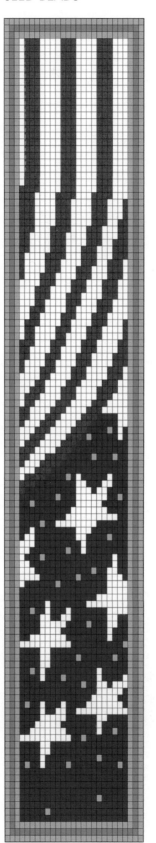

The Colors

WIDTH/11-DELICAS	1.6"	4 cm
WIDTH /15° SEED BEADS	1.35"	3.4 cm
WIDTH /11° SEED BEADS	1.7"	4.3 cm

WARP THREADS REQUIRED 28
UNITS 27 X 121

Delica 351 (925)

Delica 756 (891)

Delica 41 (608)

Delica 753 (584)

Delica 1210 (288)

Shown in 15° seed beads with three buttonholes
(placement in yellow on the chart) with firepolish
round buttons. Weave three outer rows on both ends
before beginning; start at buttonhole end and continued until the desired length is achieved

Unbeaded buttonhole locations
shown in yellow

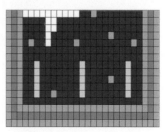

▼ START

CONTINUE

CYLINDERS

SEED BEADS

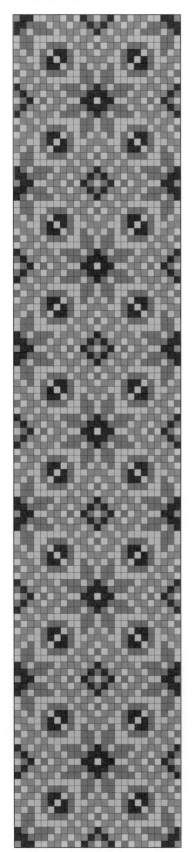

December

WIDTH/11-DELICAS	1.5″	3.7 cm
WIDTH /15° SEED BEADS	1.25″	3.2 cm
WIDTH /11° SEED BEADS	1.6″	4 cm

WARP THREADS REQUIRED 26
UNITS 25 X 121

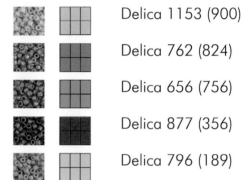

Delica 1153 (900)

Delica 762 (824)

Delica 656 (756)

Delica 877 (356)

Delica 796 (189)

Matte colors, especially matte metallic colors are highly recommended for this design

THIS ENLARGED CHART SHOWS HALF OF THIS REPEATING MOTIF DESIGN;
TO COMPLETE THE DESIGN, REPEAT FROM THE START POINT TO THE DESIRED
LENGTH. **DO NOT REPEAT THE CENTER ROW (OUTLINED IN RED)**

▼ START

CENTER ROW

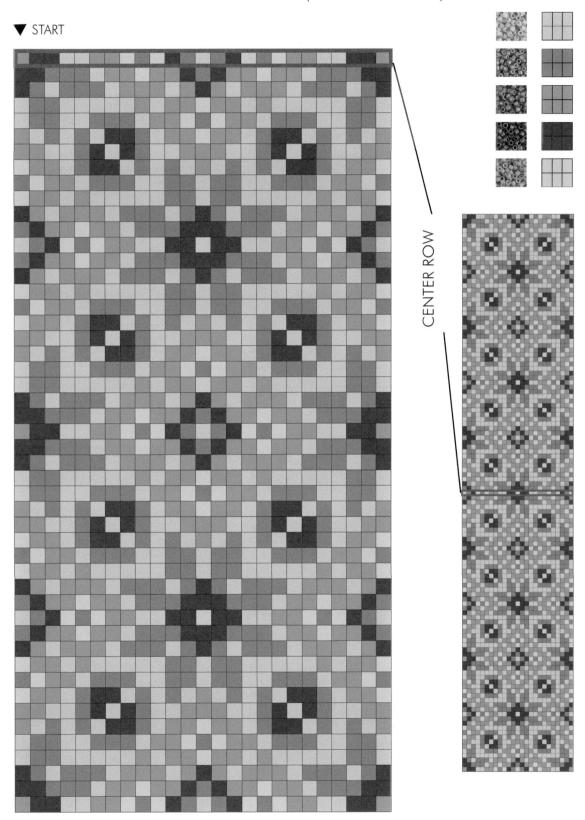

CYLINDERS   SEED BEADS

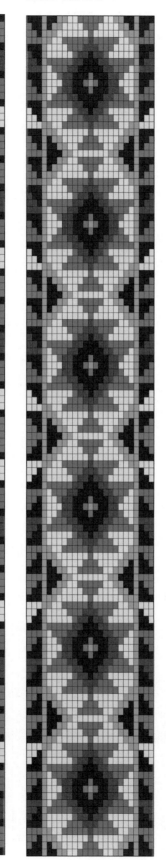

Delano

WIDTH/11-DELICAS	1.5"	3.7 cm
WIDTH /15° SEED BEADS	1.25"	3.2 cm
WIDTH /11° SEED BEADS	1.6"	4 cm

WARP THREADS REQUIRED 26
UNITS 25 X 119

Delica 1511 (767)

Delica 310 (667)

Delica 755 (612)

Delica 206 (432)

Delica 2288 (336)

Delica 729 (96)

Delica 758 (66)

THIS ENLARGED CHART SHOWS HALF OF THE DESIGN; START AT THE CENTER POINT OF THE LOOM AND WORK OUTWARD FROM THE CENTER ROW **(OUTLINED IN RED).** ROTATE THE LOOM OR CHART AND WEAVE THE OTHER HALF OF THE DESIGN, **BUT DO NOT REPEAT THE CENTER ROW.**

▼ START

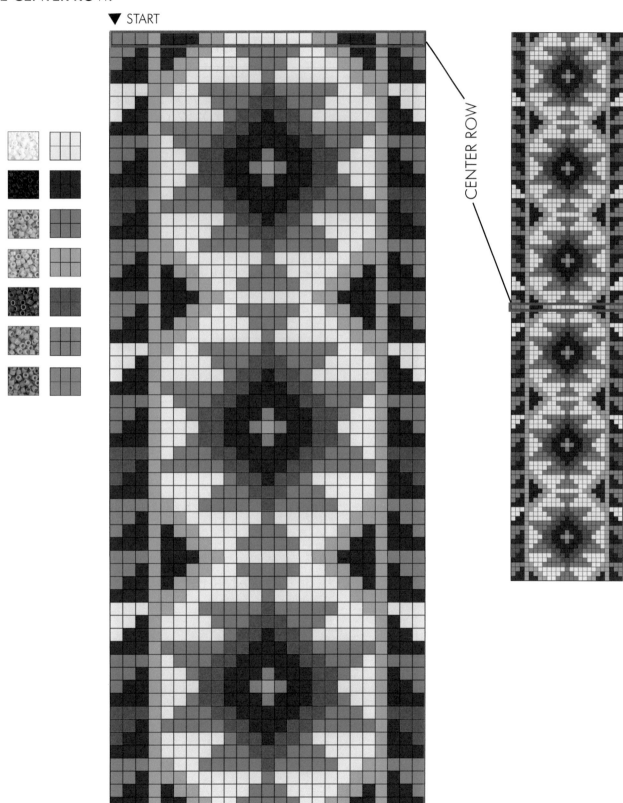

CENTER ROW

CYLINDERS   SEEDBEADS

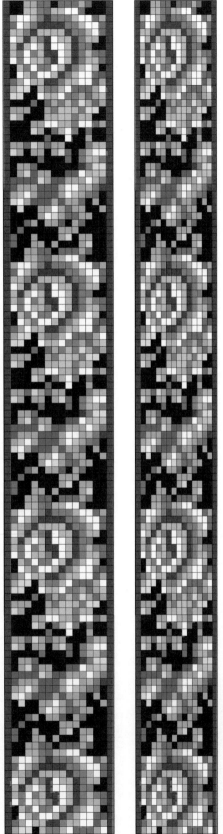

Floral

WIDTH/11-DELICAS	.95"	2.4 cm
WIDTH /15° SEEDBEADS	.8"	2.1 cm
WIDTH /11° SEEDBEADS	1"	2.5 cm

WARP THREADS REQUIRED 17
UNITS 16 X 120

Delica 756 (392)

Delica 757 (334)

Delica 1522 (248)

Delica 352 (191)

Delica 872 (179)

Delica 877 (152)

Delica 876 (91)

Delica 356 (85)

Delica 1597 (81)

Delica 758 (71)

Delica 1596 (68)

Delica 1592 (28)

START ▶

CONTINUE

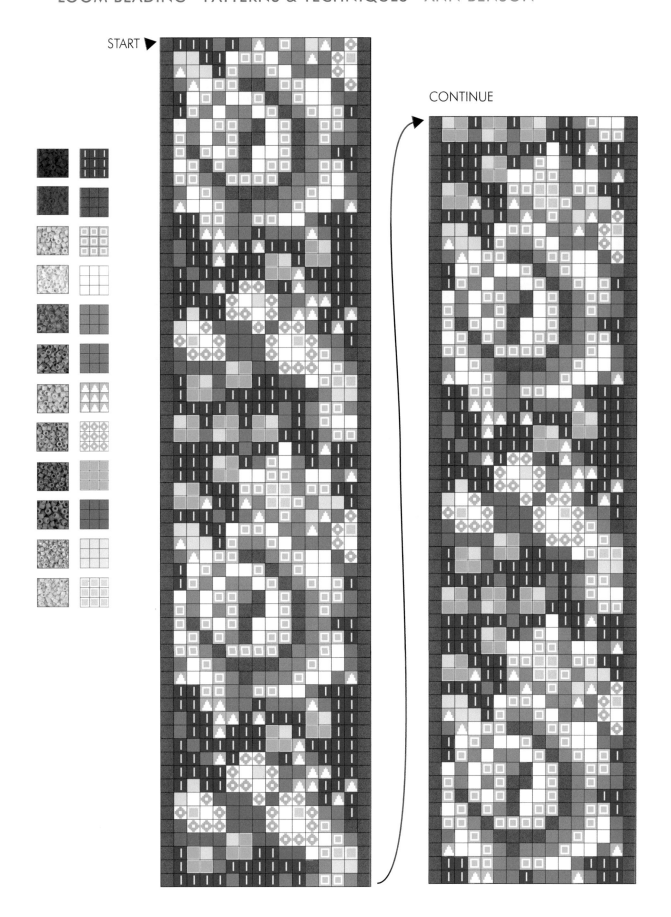

CYLINDERS   SEED BEADS

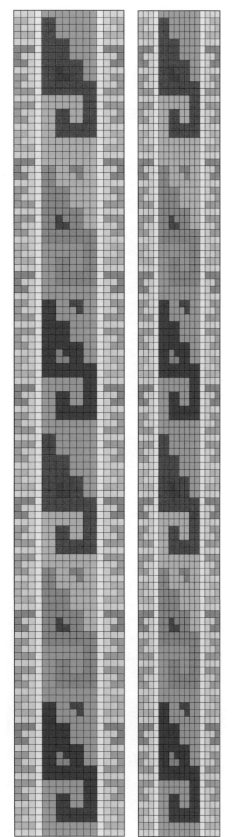

Frets

WIDTH/11-DELICAS	.95"	2.4 cm
WIDTH /15° SEED BEADS	.8"	2.1 cm
WIDTH /11° SEED BEADS	1"	2.5 cm

WARP THREADS REQUIRED 17
UNITS 16 X 117

Delica 1591 (354)

Delica 2133 (152)

Delica 881 (236)

Delica 2112 (236)

Delica 352 (234)

Delica 1136 (258)

Delica 757 (158)

Delica 1597 (152)

Delica 758 (90)

Loops are made
from 15° seed beads

▼ START

CONTINUE

CYLINDERS SEEDBEADS

WIDTH/11-DELICAS	1.7"	4.3 cm
WIDTH /15° SEEDBEADS	1.45"	3.7 cm
WIDTH /11° SEEDBEADS	1.8"	4.6 cm

WARP THREADS REQUIRED 30
UNITS 29 X 125

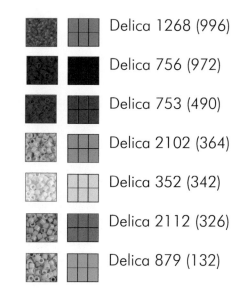

Delica 1268 (996)

Delica 756 (972)

Delica 753 (490)

Delica 2102 (364)

Delica 352 (342)

Delica 2112 (326)

Delica 879 (132)

▼ START

CENTER ROW

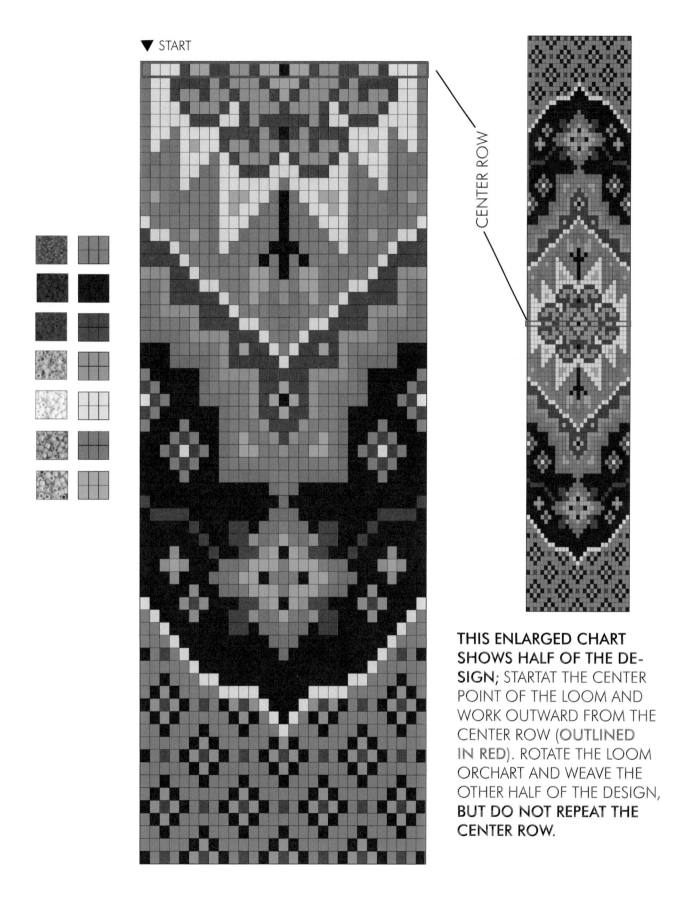

**THIS ENLARGED CHART
SHOWS HALF OF THE DE-
SIGN;** START AT THE CENTER
POINT OF THE LOOM AND
WORK OUTWARD FROM THE
CENTER ROW (**OUTLINED
IN RED**). ROTATE THE LOOM
OR CHART AND WEAVE THE
OTHER HALF OF THE DESIGN,
**BUT DO NOT REPEAT THE
CENTER ROW.**

Jewel

CYLINDERS

SEED BEADS

WIDTH/11-DELICAS	2.2"	5.7 cm
WIDTH /15° SEED BEADS	1.45"	3.7 cm
WIDTH /11° SEED BEADS	2.3"	5.9 cm

WARP THREADS REQUIRED 38
UNITS 37 X 126

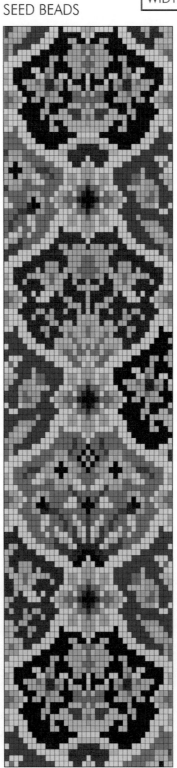

Delica 374 (1017)

Delica 2140 (694)

Delica 2136 (654)

Delica 1514 (640)

Delica 1376 (528)

Delica 327 (520)

Delica 2102 (262)

Delica 858 (247)

SHOWN STITCHED IN 11° SEED BEADS ON #14
INTERLOCK NEEDLEPOINT CANVAS

46

▼ START

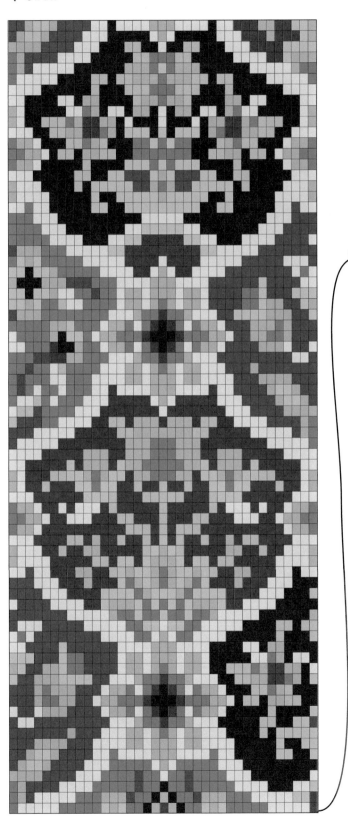

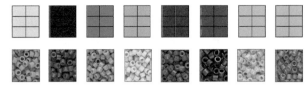

CONTINUE

CYLINDERS

SEED BEADS

WIDTH/11-DELICAS	1.6"	4 cm
WIDTH /15° SEED BEADS	1.35"	3.5 cm
WIDTH /11° SEED BEADS	1.7"	4.3 cm

WARP THREADS REQUIRED 28
UNITS 27 X 121

Delica 377 (936)

Delica 881 (95)

Delica 1517 (144)

Delica 1379 (192)

Delica 2136 (188)

Delica 1522 (234)

Delica 872 (214)

Delica 753 (116)

Delica 655 (252)

Delica 733 (275)

Shown here woven in 11° seed beads
with loop and pearl closure and single
bead edge decoration

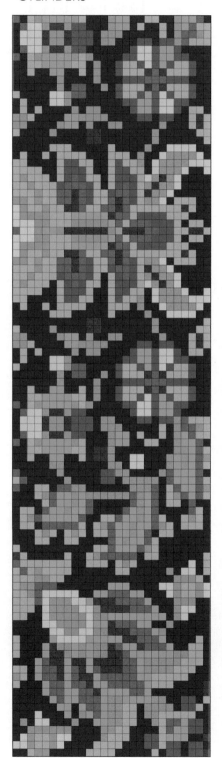

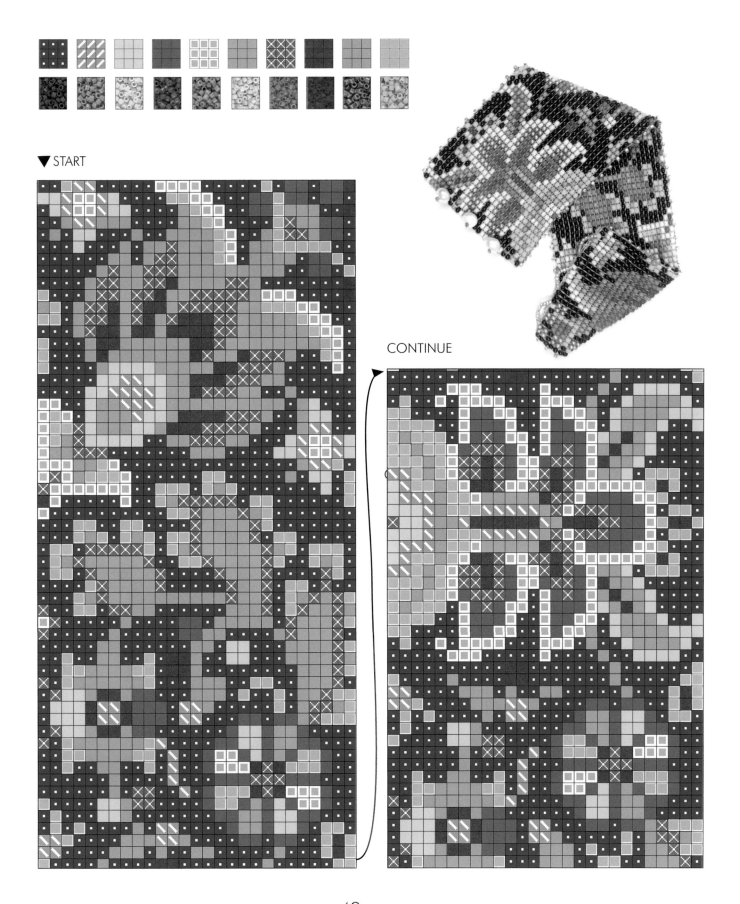

▼ START

CONTINUE

Kazak

CYLINDERS   SEED BEADS

WIDTH/11-DELICAS	1.6"	4 cm
WIDTH /15° SEED BEADS	1.35"	3.5 cm
WIDTH /11° SEED BEADS	1.7"	4.3 cm

WARP THREADS REQUIRED 38
UNITS 27 X 97

Delica 352 (1052)

Delica 377 (412)

Delica 655 (256)

Delica 875 (253)

Delica 1832F (248)

Delica 2133 (196)

Delica 753 (158)

Delica 1496 (44)

Shown here in 11° seed
beads with loop and bead
closure and single bead edge
decoration

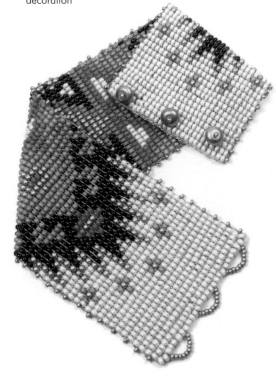

THIS ENLARGED CHART SHOWS HALF OF THIS MIRRORED DESIGN; START AT THE CENTER POINT OF THE LOOM AND WORK OUTWARD FROM THE CENTER ROW (**OUTLINED IN RED**).

▼ START

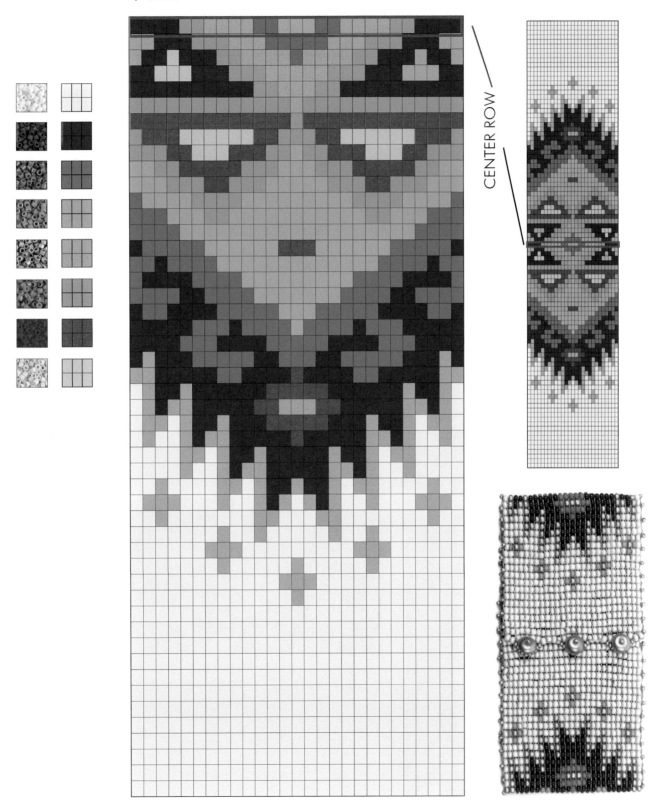

CENTER ROW

CYLINDERS   SEED BEADS

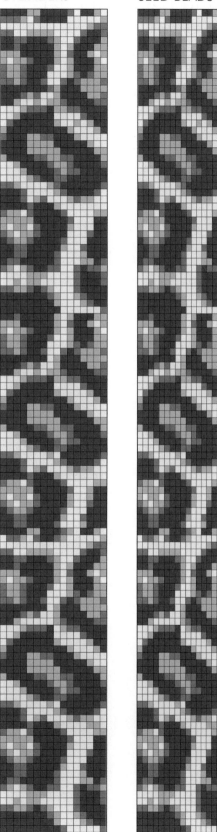

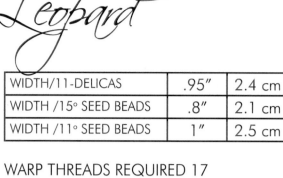

Leopard

WIDTH/11-DELICAS	.95"	2.4 cm
WIDTH /15° SEED BEADS	.8"	2.1 cm
WIDTH /11° SEED BEADS	1"	2.5 cm

WARP THREADS REQUIRED 17
UNITS 16 x 119 ROWS

Delica 762 (802)

Delica 866 (422)

Delica 2286 (380)

Delica 1910 (300)

▼ START

CONTINUE

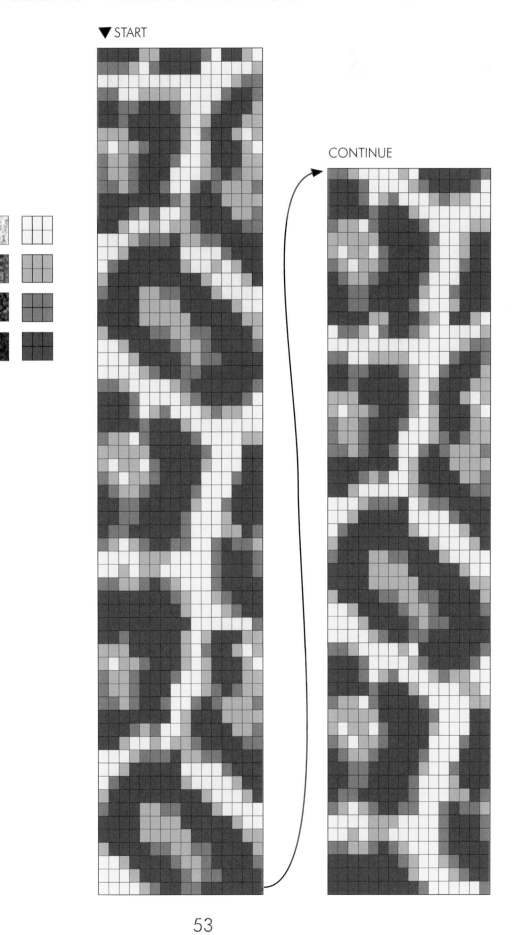

CYLINDERS

SEED BEADS

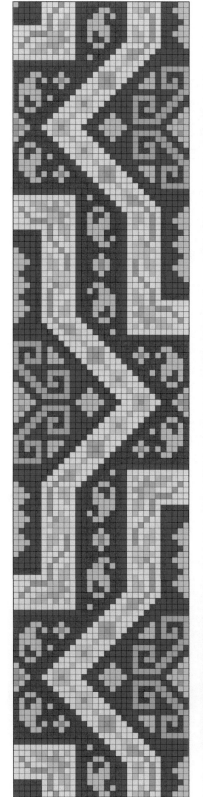

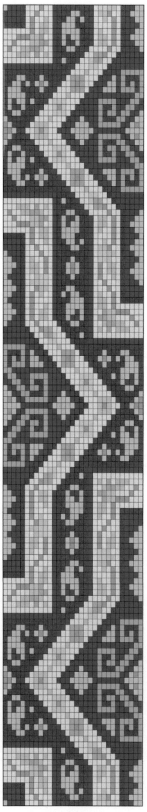

WIDTH/11-DELICAS	1.8"	4.6 cm
WIDTH /15° SEED BEADS	1.55"	3.9 cm
WIDTH /11° SEED BEADS	1.9"	4.9 cm

WARP THREADS REQUIRED 32
UNITS 31 x 137

Delica 756 (990)

Delica 2352 (956)

Delica 352 (946)

Delica 374 (441)

Delica 1363 (242)

Delica 2285 (223)

Delica 793 (162)

Delica 1517 (86)

THIS ENLARGED CHART SHOWS HALF OF THIS MIRRORED DESIGN; START AT THE CENTER
POINT OF THE LOOM AND WORK OUTWARD FROM THE CENTER ROW (**OUTLINED IN RED**).

▼ START

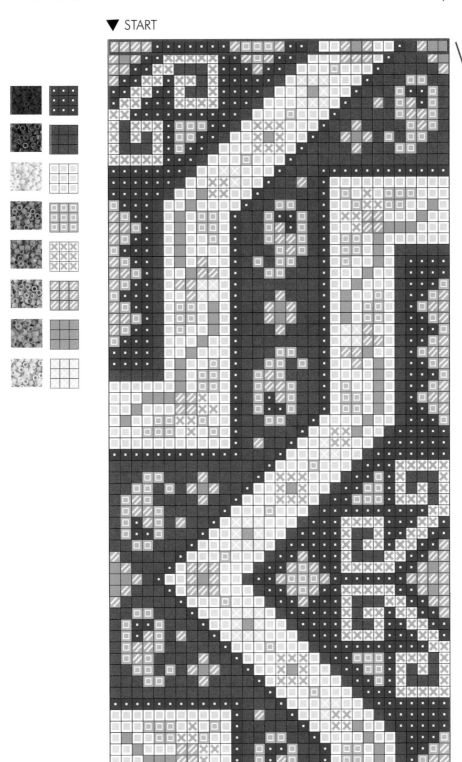

CENTER ROW

CYLINDERS   SEED BEADS

WIDTH/11-DELICAS	1.35"	3.4 cm
WIDTH /15° SEED BEADS	1.15"	2.9 cm
WIDTH /11° SEED BEADS	1.44"	3.7 cm

WARP THREADS REQUIRED 24
UNITS 23 x 127

Delica 729 (776)

Delica 352 (732)

Delica 2143 (462)

Delica 2290 (411)

Delica 2291 (336)

Delica 356 (204)

START ▶

THIS ENLARGED CHART SHOWS HALF OF THIS MIR-RORED DESIGN; START AT THE CENTER POINT OF THE LOOM AND WORK OUT-WARD FROM THE CENTER ROW (**OUTLINED IN RED**).

CENTER ROW

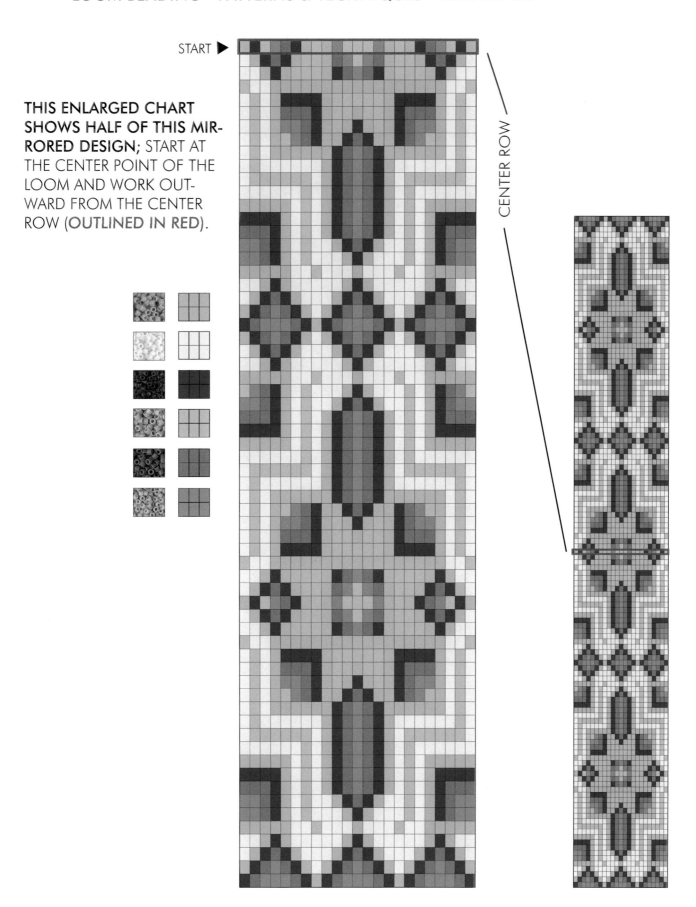

Orientale

CYLINDERS   SEED BEADS

WIDTH/11-DELICAS	2.2"	5.5 cm
WIDTH /15° SEED BEADS	1.85"	4.7 cm
WIDTH /11° SEED BEADS	2.3"	5.9 cm

WARP THREADS REQUIRED 38
UNITS 37 X 125

Delica 310 (1495)

Delica 2133 (994)

Delica 356 (792)

Delica 1832 (645)

Delica 352 (365)

Delica 728 (247)

Delica 2118 (87)

Shown here is 15° seed beads for a 6" wrist.
The closure is buttonholes with seven freshwater pearls. The edge is undecorated.

THIS ENLARGED CHART SHOWS HALF OF THIS MIRRORED DESIGN; START AT THE CENTER POINT OF THE LOOM AND WORK OUTWARD FROM THE CENTER ROW (**OUTLINED IN RED**).

▼ START

Shown here is 15° seed beads for a 6" wrist. The closure is buttonholes with seven freshwater pearls. The edge is undecorated.

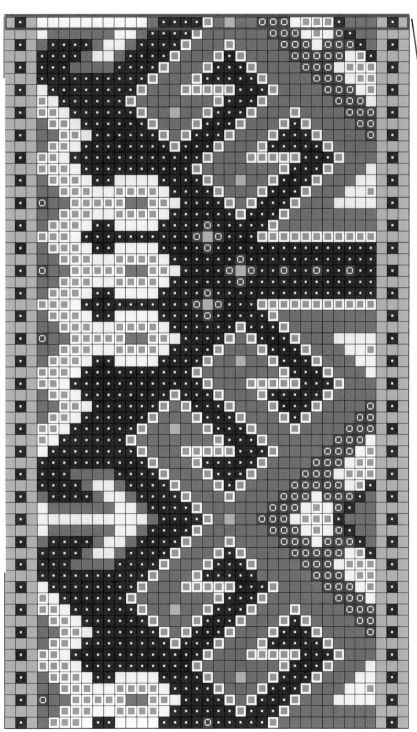

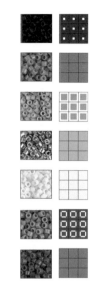

CENTER ROW

CYLINDERS   SEED BEADS

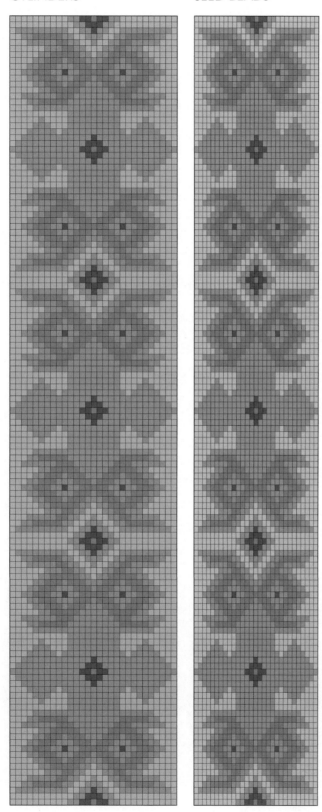

Owl Eyes

WIDTH/11-DELICAS	1.7"	4.3 cm
WIDTH /15° SEED BEADS	1.45"	3.7 cm
WIDTH /11° SEED BEADS	1.8"	4.6 cm

WARP THREADS REQUIRED 30
UNITS 29 x 133

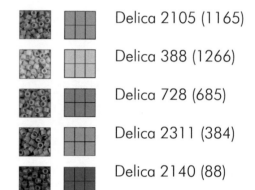

Delica 2105 (1165)

Delica 388 (1266)

Delica 728 (685)

Delica 2311 (384)

Delica 2140 (88)

▼ START

THIS ENLARGED CHART SHOWS HALF OF THIS MIRRORED DESIGN; START AT THE CENTER POINT OF THE LOOM AND WORK OUTWARD FROM THE CENTER ROW (OUTLINED IN RED).

CENTER ROW

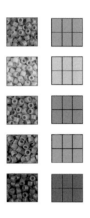

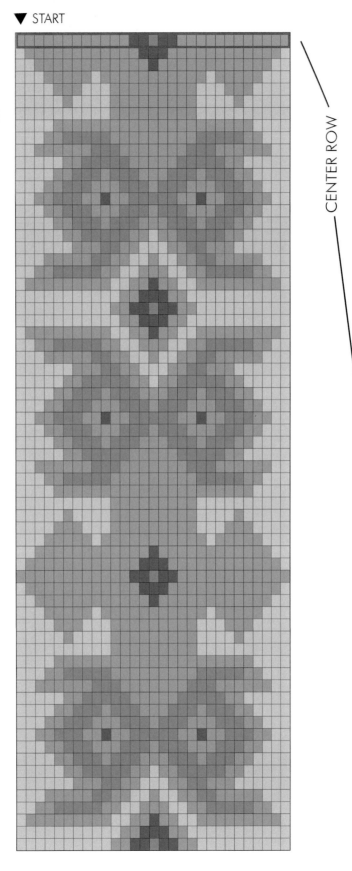

Paisley

CYLINDERS   SEED BEADS

WIDTH/11-DELICAS	1.8"	4.6 cm
WIDTH /15° SEED BEADS	1.55"	3.9 cm
WIDTH /11° SEED BEADS	1.9"	4.9 cm

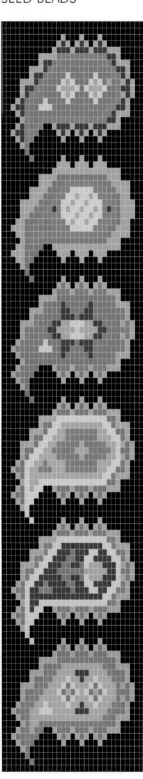

WARP THREADS REQUIRED 32
UNITS 31 x 118

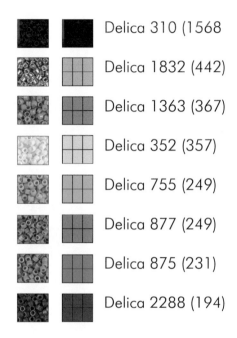

Delica 310 (1568

Delica 1832 (442)

Delica 1363 (367)

Delica 352 (357)

Delica 755 (249)

Delica 877 (249)

Delica 875 (231)

Delica 2288 (194)

Shown here in 15° seed beads. The ends are woven in simple over-under weave in size 10 perle cotton, with three buttonholes. The buttons are crystal rondelles. Edges are decorated with single seed beads.

▼ START

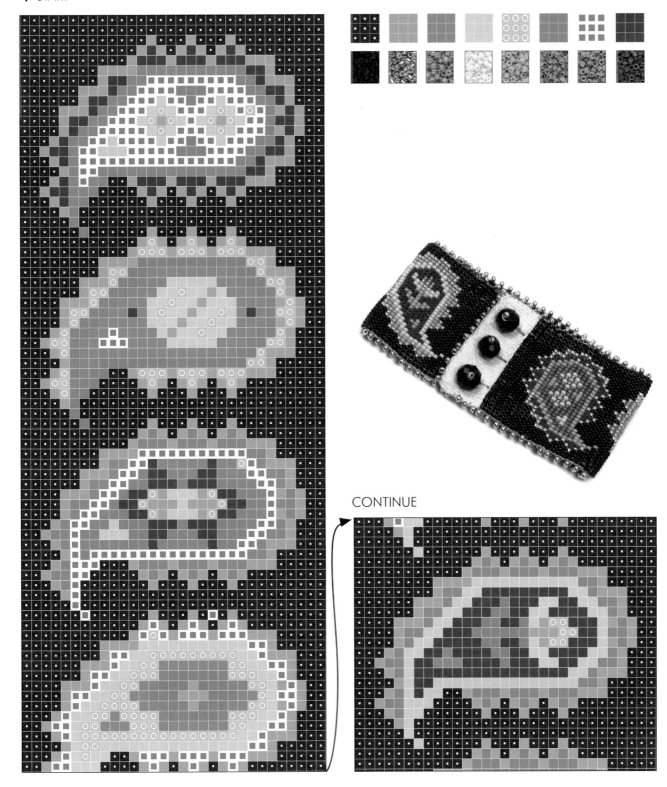

CONTINUE

CYLINDERS

SEED BEADS

Persian

WIDTH/11-DELICAS	1.35"	3.4 cm
WIDTH /15° SEED BEADS	1.2"	2.9 cm
WIDTH /11° SEED BEADS	1.44"	3.7 cm

WARP THREADS REQUIRED 24
UNITS 23 x 121

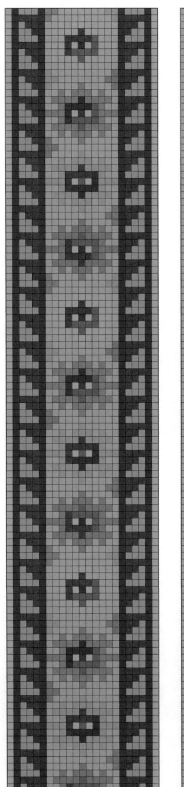

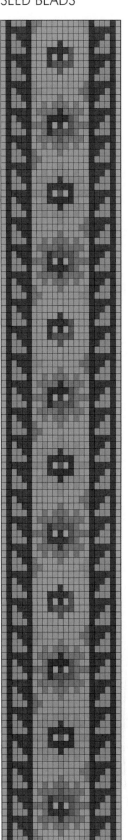

Delica 1591 (571)

Delica 2143 (532)

Delica 2309 (506)

Delica 753 (426)

Delica 793 (380)

Delica 855 (140)

Delica 758 (138)

Delica 656 (66)

Delica 2285 (24)

Shown here in 15° seed beads with loop and
bead closure and a single bead edging

▼ START

CONTINUE

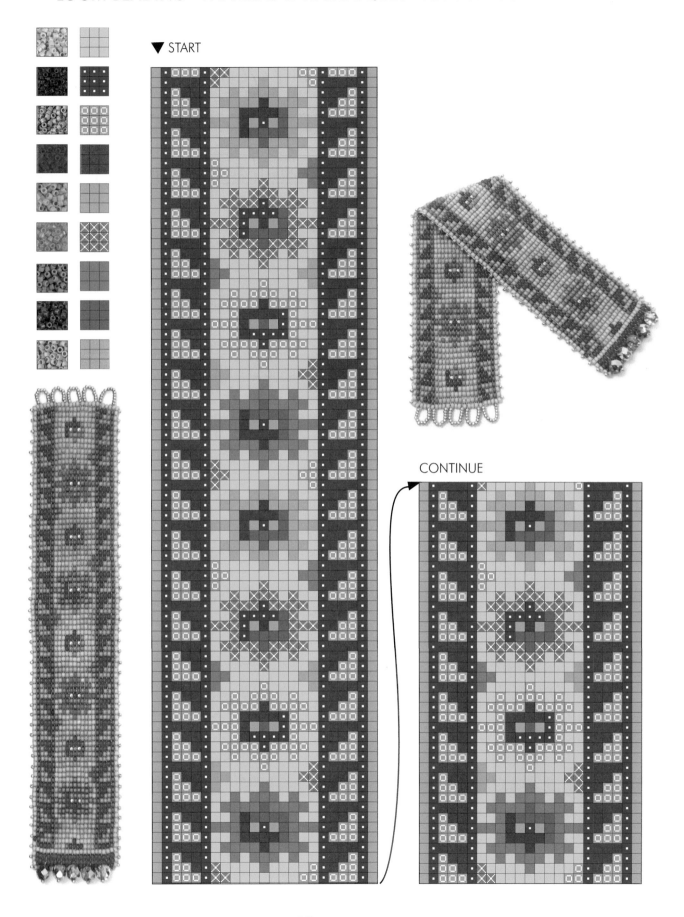

CYLINDERS   SEED BEADS

WIDTH/11-DELICAS	1.5"	3.7 cm
WIDTH /15° SEED BEADS	1.25"	3.2 cm
WIDTH /11° SEED BEADS	1.6"	4 cm

WARP THREADS REQUIRED 26
UNITS 25 x 125

Delica 2102 (1101)

Delica 722 (831)

Delica 793 (687)

Delica 2139 (506)

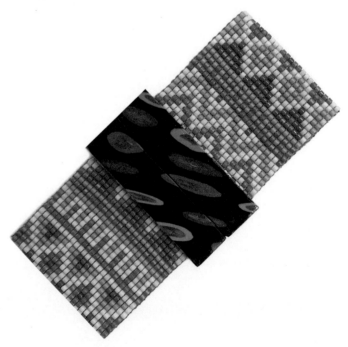

Shown in size 11 Delicas with a magnetic clasp
finished with a polymer clay layer.

66

▼ START

CONTINUE

CYLINDERS

SEED BEADS

Purple Sage

WIDTH/11-DELICAS	1.25"	3.1cm
WIDTH /15° SEED BEADS	1.1"	2.8cm
WIDTH /11° SEED BEADS	1.3"	3.3cm

WARP THREADS REQUIRED 22
UNITS 21 X 127

Delica 2136 (768)

Delica 1154 (694)

Delica 2293 (491)

Delica 2357 (360)

Delica 352 (354)

▼ START

THIS ENLARGED CHART SHOWS HALF OF THIS MIRRORED DESIGN; START AT THE CENTER POINT OF THE LOOM AND WORK OUTWARD FROM THE CENTER ROW (OUTLINED IN RED). ROTATE THE LOOM OR CHART AND WEAVE THE OTHER HALF OF THE DESIGN, **BUT DO NOT REPEAT THE CENTER ROW.**

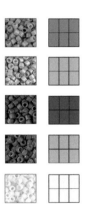

CENTER ROW

CYLINDERS   SEED BEADS

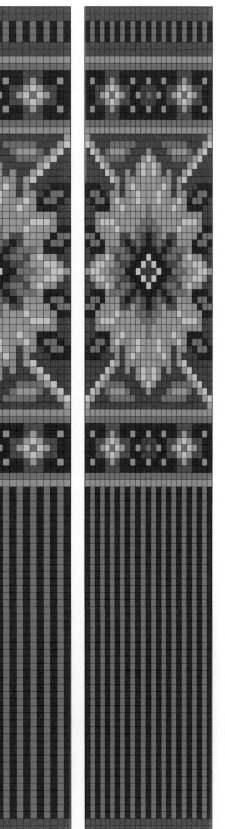

WIDTH/11-DELICAS	1.5"	3.7 cm
WIDTH /15° SEED BEADS	1.25"	3.2 cm
WIDTH /11° SEED BEADS	1.6"	4 cm

WARP THREADS REQUIRED 26
UNITS 25 X ADJUSTABLE LENGTH

Delica 2143 (933)

Delica 877 (776)

Delica 757 (281)

Delica 2110 (280)

Delica 1586 (270)

Delica 1582 (211)

Delica 1511 (116)

Delica 2112 (56)

Shown here in 11° seed beads sized for a 6.5" wrist with buttonhole
closure and metal rondelle buttons. The edging is a three-bead picot.

▼ START

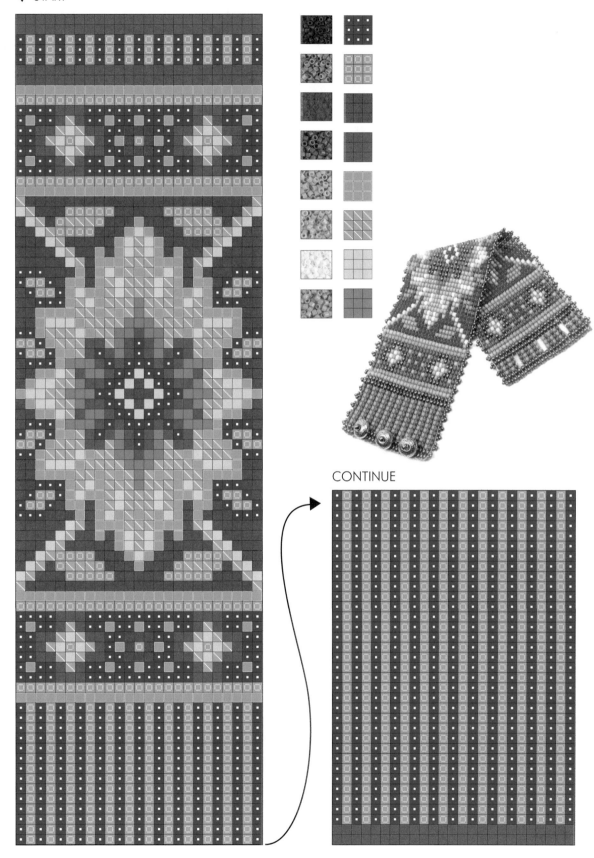

CONTINUE

Senna

CYLINDERS   **SEED BEADS**

WIDTH/11-DELICAS	2"	5.2 cm
WIDTH /15° SEED BEADS	1.75"	4.5 cm
WIDTH /11° SEED BEADS	2.2"	5.6 cm

WARP THREADS REQUIRED 36
UNITS 35 X 131 ROWS

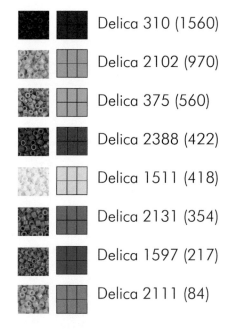

Delica 310 (1560)

Delica 2102 (970)

Delica 375 (560)

Delica 2388 (422)

Delica 1511 (418)

Delica 2131 (354)

Delica 1597 (217)

Delica 2111 (84)

▼ START

CONTINUE

CYLINDERS   **SEED BEADS**

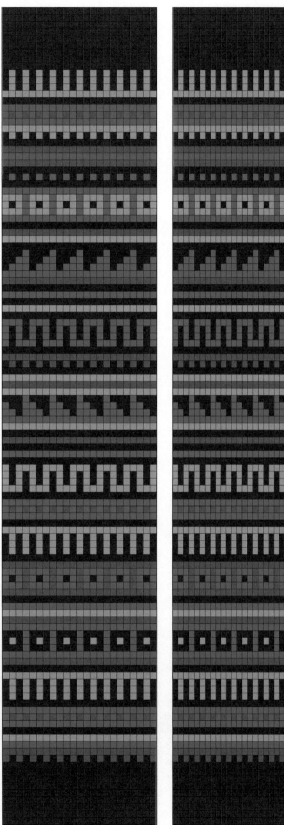

WIDTH/11-DELICAS	1.35"	3.4 cm
WIDTH /15° SEED BEADS	1.15"	2.9 cm
WIDTH /11° SEED BEADS	1.44"	3.7 cm

WARP THREADS REQUIRED 24
UNITS 23 x 120 ROWS

 Delica 2143 (1236)

 Delica 1597 (595)

Delica 752 (558)

Delica 2885 (446)

Shown here in 15° seed beads sized for a 6.5" wrist.
The closure has three buttonholes and three freshwater
pearls. The edging is a single bead picot.

▼ START

CONTINUE

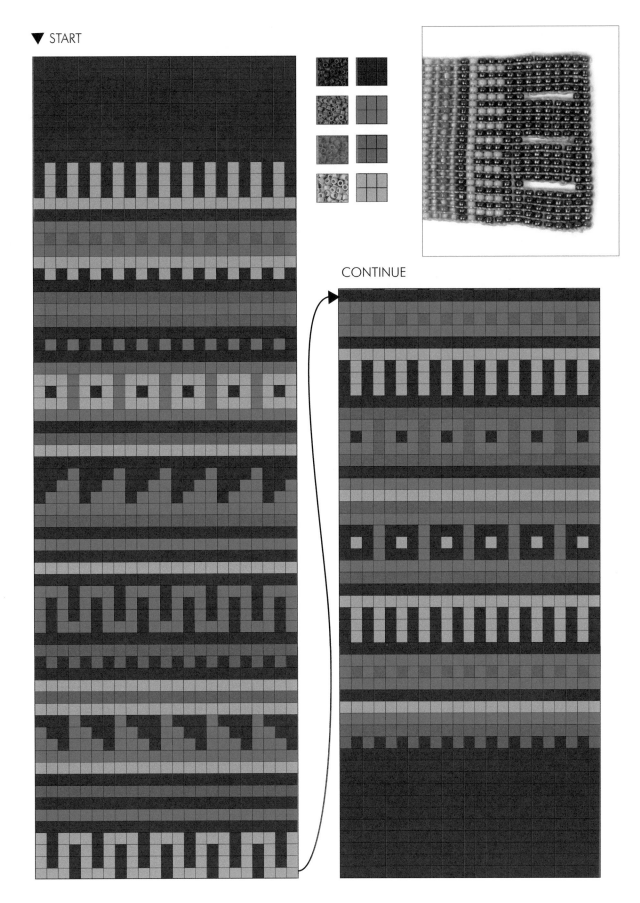

CYLINDERS

SEED BEADS

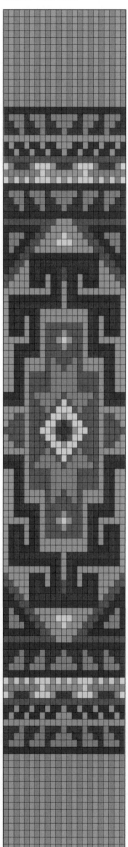

Shirvan

WIDTH/11-DELICAS	1.5"	3.7 cm
WIDTH /15° SEED BEADS	1.25"	3.2 cm
WIDTH /11° SEED BEADS	1.6"	4 cm

WARP THREADS REQUIRED 24
UNITS 23 X 121 ROWS

Delica 879 (630)

Delica 2290 (616)

Delica 2143 (516)

Delica 753 (345)

Delica 855 (258)

Delica 2103 (208)

Delica 877 (122)

Delica 1502 (86)

Shown here woven in 11° seed beads. Three firepolish rondelles are used as button for the 15° seed bead loops. Edges are decorated with 8° and 15° seed beads.

76

▼ START

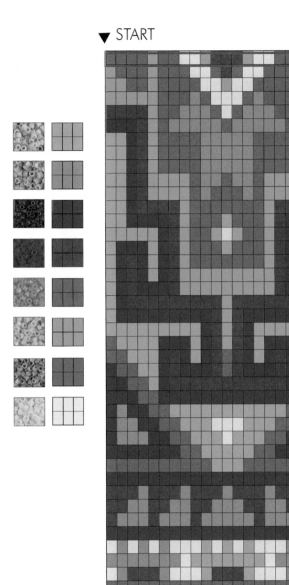

THIS ENLARGED CHART SHOWS HALF OF THIS MIRRORED DESIGN; START AT THE CENTER POINT OF THE LOOM AND WORK OUTWARD FROM THE CENTER ROW (**OUTLINED IN RED**). ROTATE THE LOOM OR CHART AND WEAVE THE OTHER HALF OF THE DESIGN, **BUT DO NOT REPEAT THE CENTER ROW.**

CENTER ROW

8°s and 15°s over every pair of edge beads

CYLINDERS

SEED BEADS

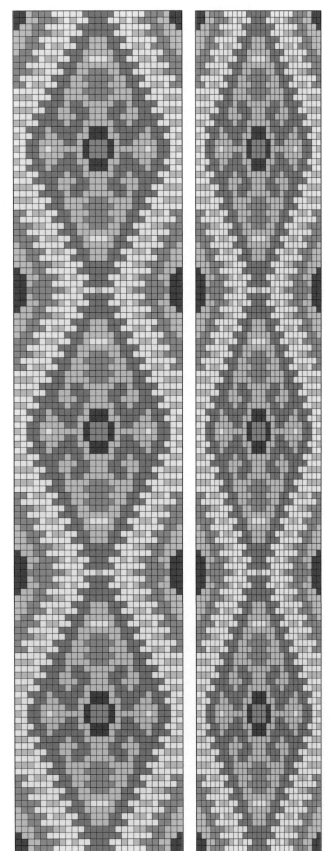

Sierra

WIDTH/11-DELICAS	1.6"	4 cm
WIDTH /15° SEED BEADS	1.35"	3.5 cm
WIDTH /11° SEED BEADS	1.7"	4.3 cm

WARP THREADS REQUIRED 28
UNITS 27 x 131 ROWS

Delica 352 (918)

Delica 2139 (912)

Delica 374 (792)

Delica 659 (525)

Delica 388 (268)

Delica 880 (122)

Shown here in 11° seed beads for a 6.5" wrist. The closure is a magnetic clasp wrapped in peyote stitch, with a bezeled stone mounted on one side of the clasp, so that when closed it appears to be centered on both sides. Both ends of the woven strip have three rows in the background color; this is woven prior to starting at the center and working outward toward the ends. The three rows are glued into the clasp; padding with a thin strip of non-woven may be needed to create a strong fit within the clasp opening.

▼ START

THIS ENLARGED CHART SHOWS HALF OF THE MIRRORED DESIGN; START AT THE CENTER POINT OF THE LOOM AND WORK OUTWARD FROM THE CENTER ROW (**OUTLINED IN RED**). ROTATE THE LOOM OR CHART; WEAVE THE OTHER HALF, **BUT DON'T REPEAT THE CENTER ROW.**

CENTER ROW

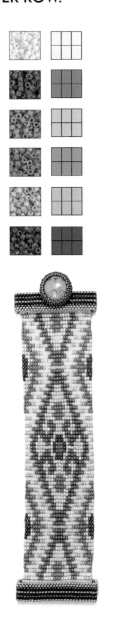

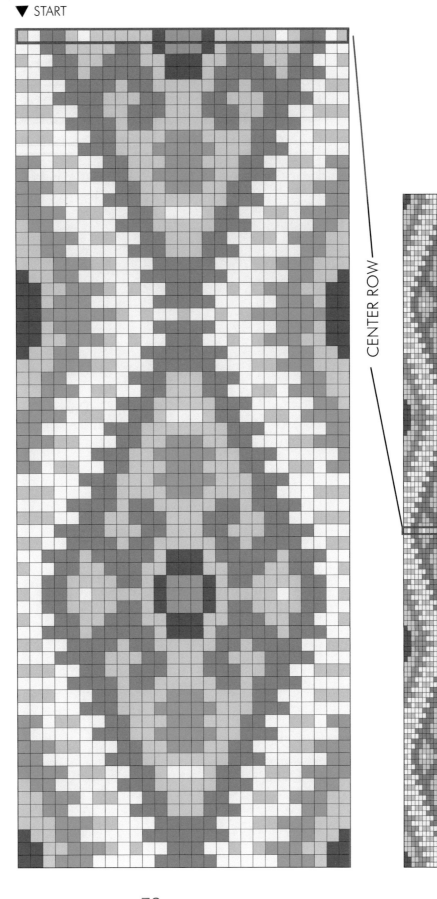

CYLINDERS

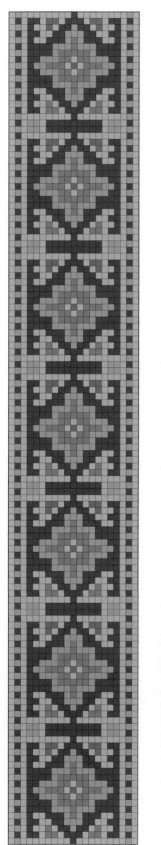

SEED BEADS

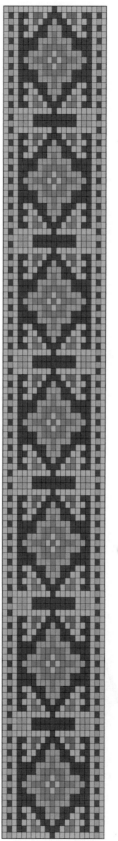

Soumak

WIDTH/11-DELICAS	1.24″	3.1 cm
WIDTH /15° SEED BEADS	1″	2.6 cm
WIDTH /11° SEED BEADS	1.3″	3.3 cm

WARP THREADS REQUIRED 22
UNITS 21 x 131 ROWS

 Delica 2125 (1024)

 Delica 2143 (952)

Delica 2111 (488)

 Delica 2131 (236)

Delica 728 (49)

Separate out one motif
and use it with fiber-
woven sides.

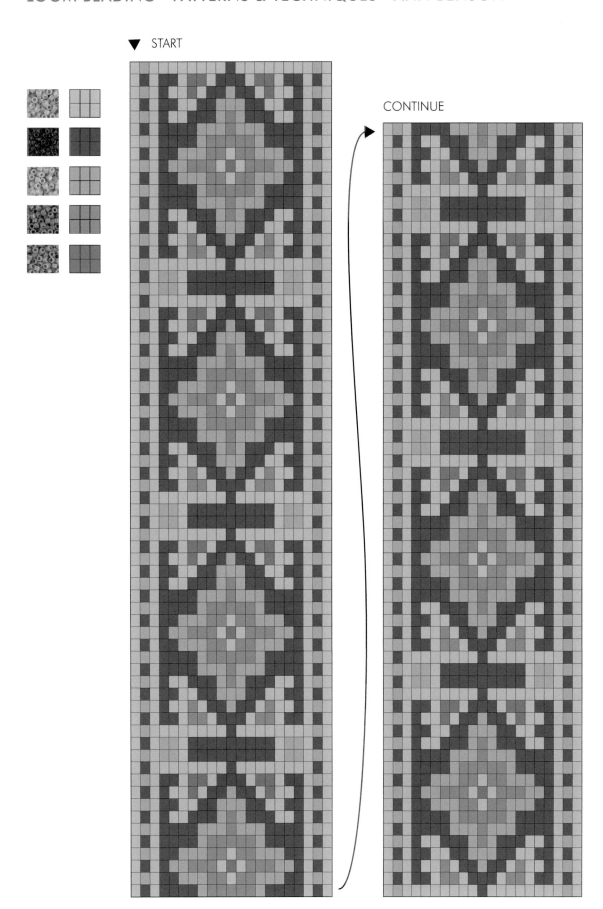

START

CONTINUE

CYLINDERS   SEED BEADS

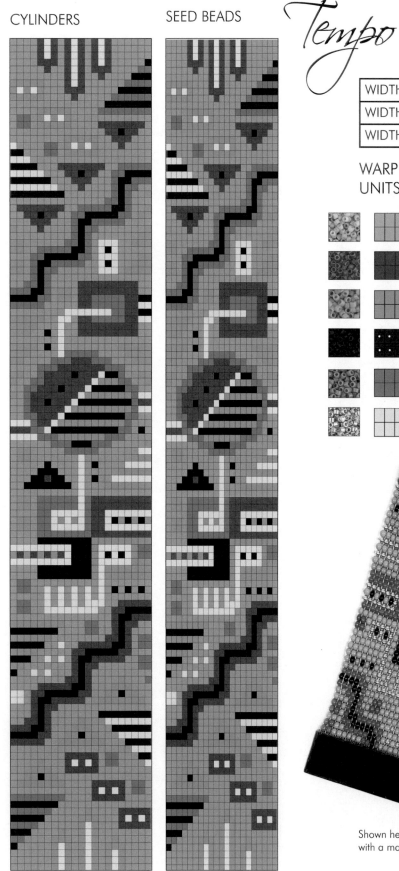

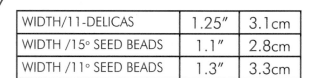

WIDTH/11-DELICAS	1.25"	3.1cm
WIDTH /15° SEED BEADS	1.1"	2.8cm
WIDTH /11° SEED BEADS	1.3"	3.3cm

WARP THREADS REQUIRED 22
UNITS 21 X 120 ROWS

Delica 1515 (1066)

Delica 873 (347)

Delica 793 (322)

Delica 301 (279)

Delica 728 (267)

Delica 1831 (239)

Shown here in 12° seed beads woven for a 7" wrist
with a magnetic clasp and no decorative edging

▼ START

CONTINUE

CYLINDERS   SEED BEADS

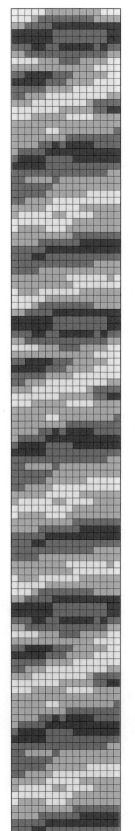

WIDTH/11-DELICAS	.94"	2.4cm
WIDTH /15° SEED BEADS	.8"	2cm
WIDTH /11° SEED BEADS	1"	2.5cm

WARP THREADS REQUIRED 17
UNITS 16 X 119 ROWS

 Delica 2286 (699)

 Delica 2288 (554)

 Delica 2101 (362)

 Delica 310 (288)

▼ START

CONTINUE

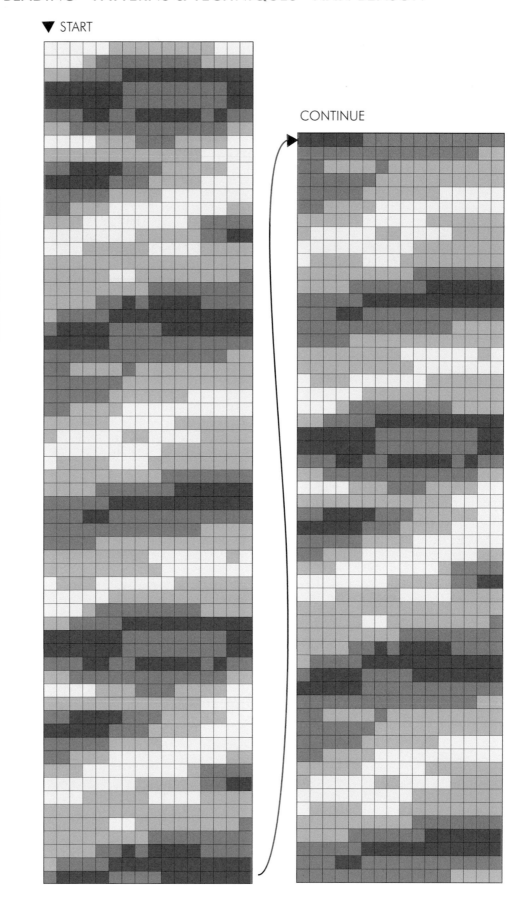

CYLINDERS

SEED BEADS

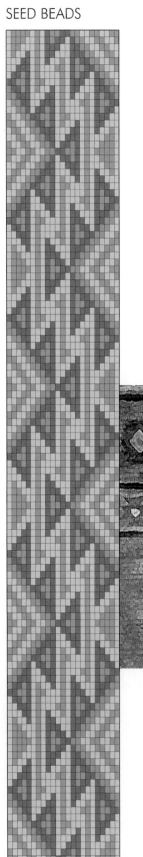

Triangulation

WIDTH/11-DELICAS	1.35"	3.4 cm
WIDTH /15° SEED BEADS	1.15"	2.9 cm
WIDTH /11° SEED BEADS	1.44"	3.7 cm

WARP THREADS REQUIRED 24
UNITS 23 X 120 ROWS

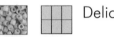 Delica 353 (1066)

 Delica 1136 (347)

 Delica 434 (322)

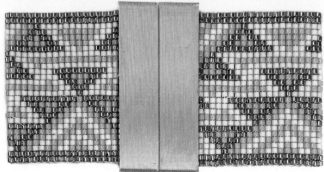

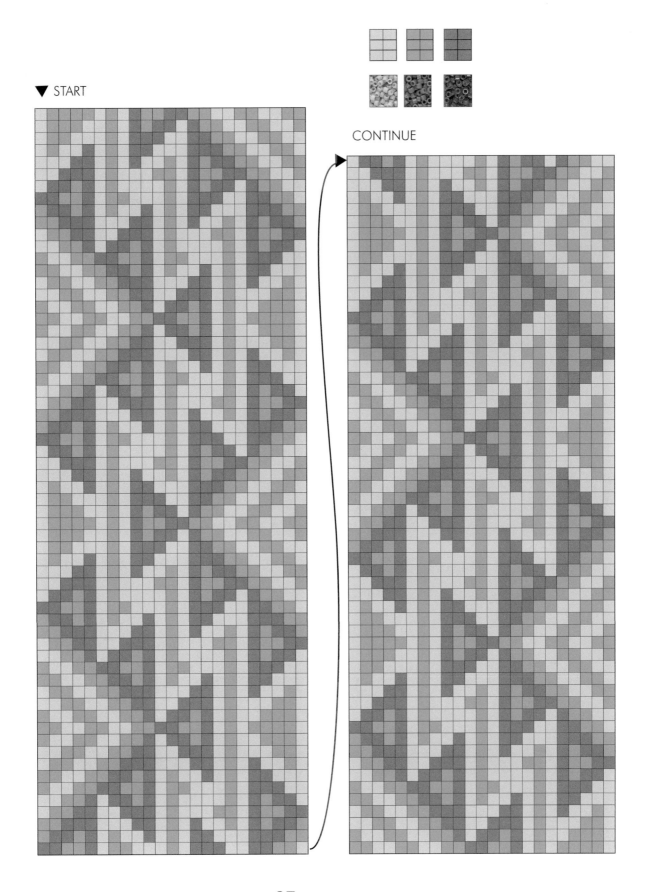

▼ START

CONTINUE

Tribal

CYLINDERS

SEED BEADS

WIDTH/11-DELICAS	2.2"	5.5 cm
WIDTH /15° SEED BEADS	1.85"	4.7 cm
WIDTH /11° SEED BEADS	2.3"	5.9 cm

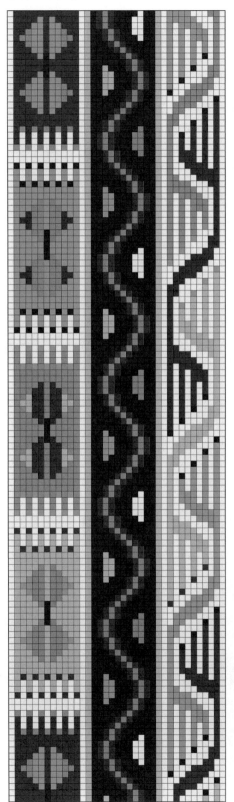

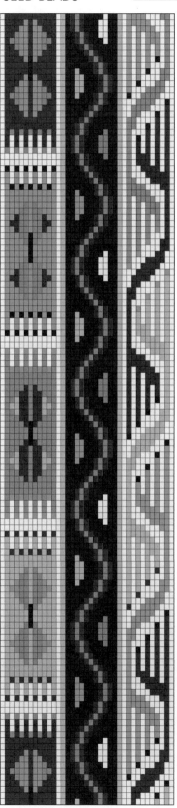

WARP THREADS REQUIRED 38
UNITS 37 X 130 ROWS

Delica 352 (1268)

Delica 310 (1003)

Delica 795 (827)

Delica 2136 (629)

Delica 2285 (576

Delica 798 (507)

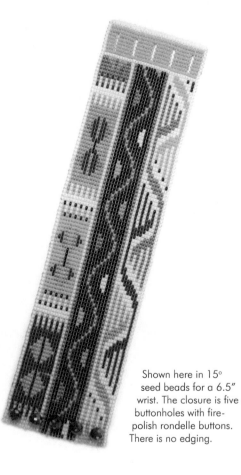

Shown here in 15°
seed beads for a 6.5"
wrist. The closure is five
buttonholes with fire-
polish rondelle buttons.
There is no edging.

▼ START

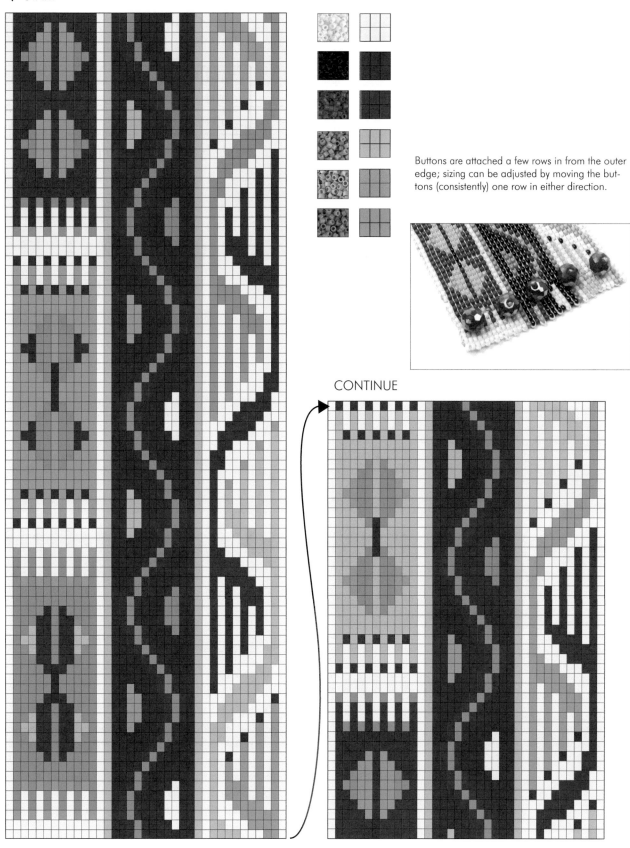

Buttons are attached a few rows in from the outer edge; sizing can be adjusted by moving the buttons (consistently) one row in either direction.

CONTINUE

CYLINDERS

SEED BEADS

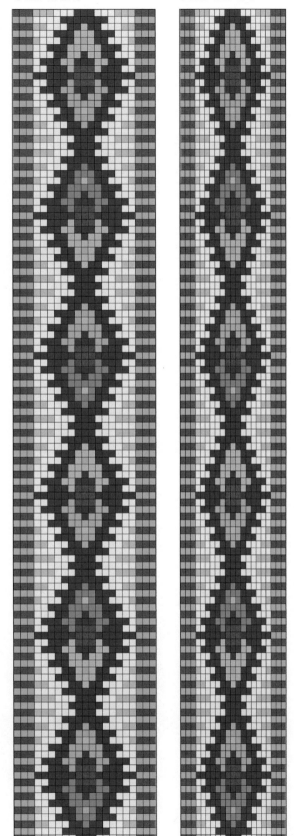

Western

WIDTH/11-DELICAS	1.25"	3.1cm
WIDTH /15° SEED BEADS	1.1"	2.8cm
WIDTH /11° SEED BEADS	1.3"	3.3cm

WARP THREADS REQUIRED 22
UNITS 21 X 119 ROWS

Delica 2317 (697)

Delica 1592 (626)

Delica 878 (442)

Delica 795 (414)

Delica 651 (235)

Delica 1587 (64)

Shown here in size 11 Delicas woven for a 6" wrist. The toggle "loop" is added to the end of the weave in square stitch, which mimics the look of looming, but allows for a cross-weave opening without warp threads. The toggle bar is created in flat peyote stitch, which is "zipped" at the edges to form a tube. The bracelet edges are undecorated. For this closure, a no-finish loom is recommended.

▼ START

CONTINUE

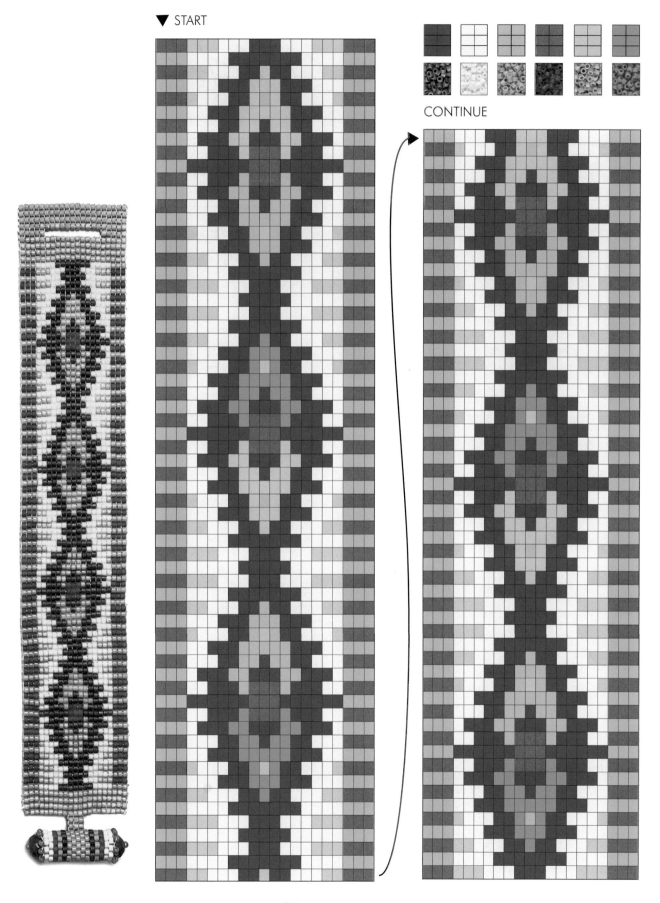

CYLINDERS

SEED BEADS

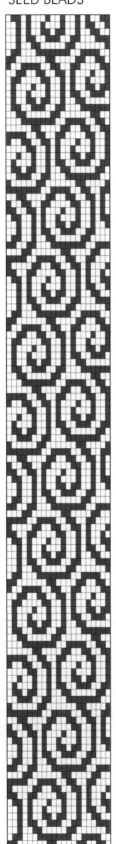

Whirls

WIDTH/11-DELICAS	1.25"	3.1cm
WIDTH /15° SEED BEADS	1.1"	2.8cm
WIDTH /11° SEED BEADS	1.3"	3.3cm

WARP THREADS REQUIRED 22
UNITS 21 X 121 ROWS

 Delica dark color (697)

 Delica light color (626)

▼ START

CONTINUE

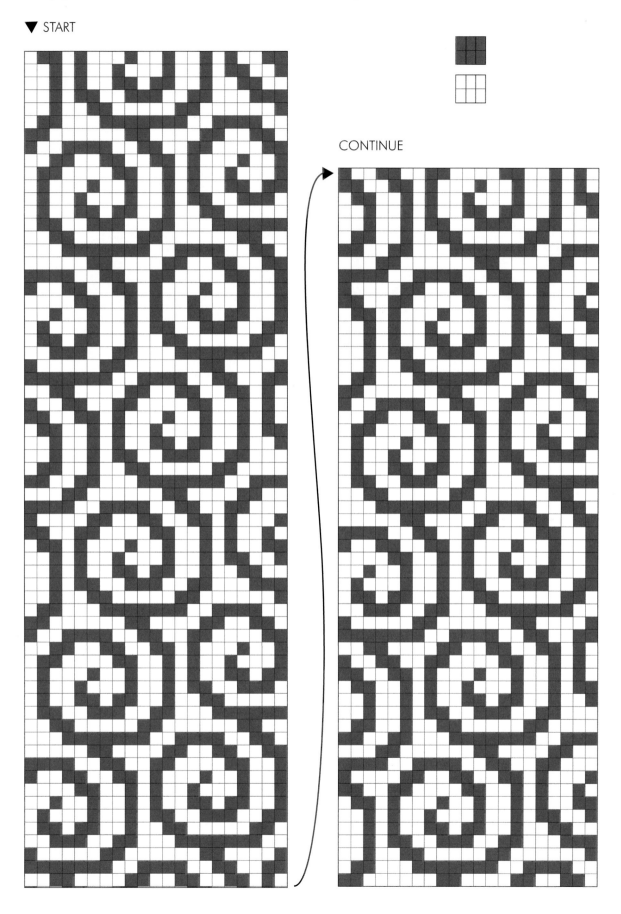

Willow

CYLINDERS   SEED BEADS

WIDTH/11-DELICAS	2.3"	5.8 cm
WIDTH /15° SEED BEADS	2"	5 cm
WIDTH /11° SEED BEADS	2.44"	6.2 cm

WARP THREADS REQUIRED 40
UNITS 39 x 120 ROWS

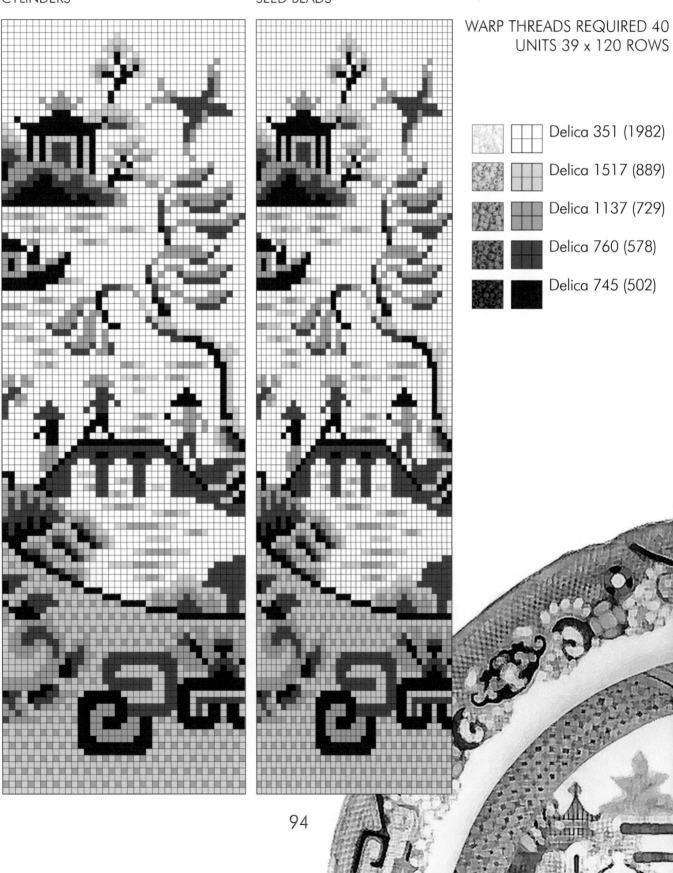

Delica 351 (1982)

Delica 1517 (889)

Delica 1137 (729)

Delica 760 (578)

Delica 745 (502)

▼ START   READ ROWS LEFT TO RIGHT, TOP TO BOTTOM, CONTINUE ON NEXT PAGE

CONTINUE

WILLOW

Enlarged chart upper portion

Continued on next page

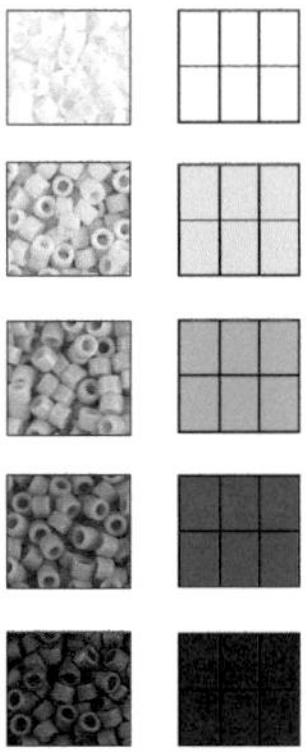

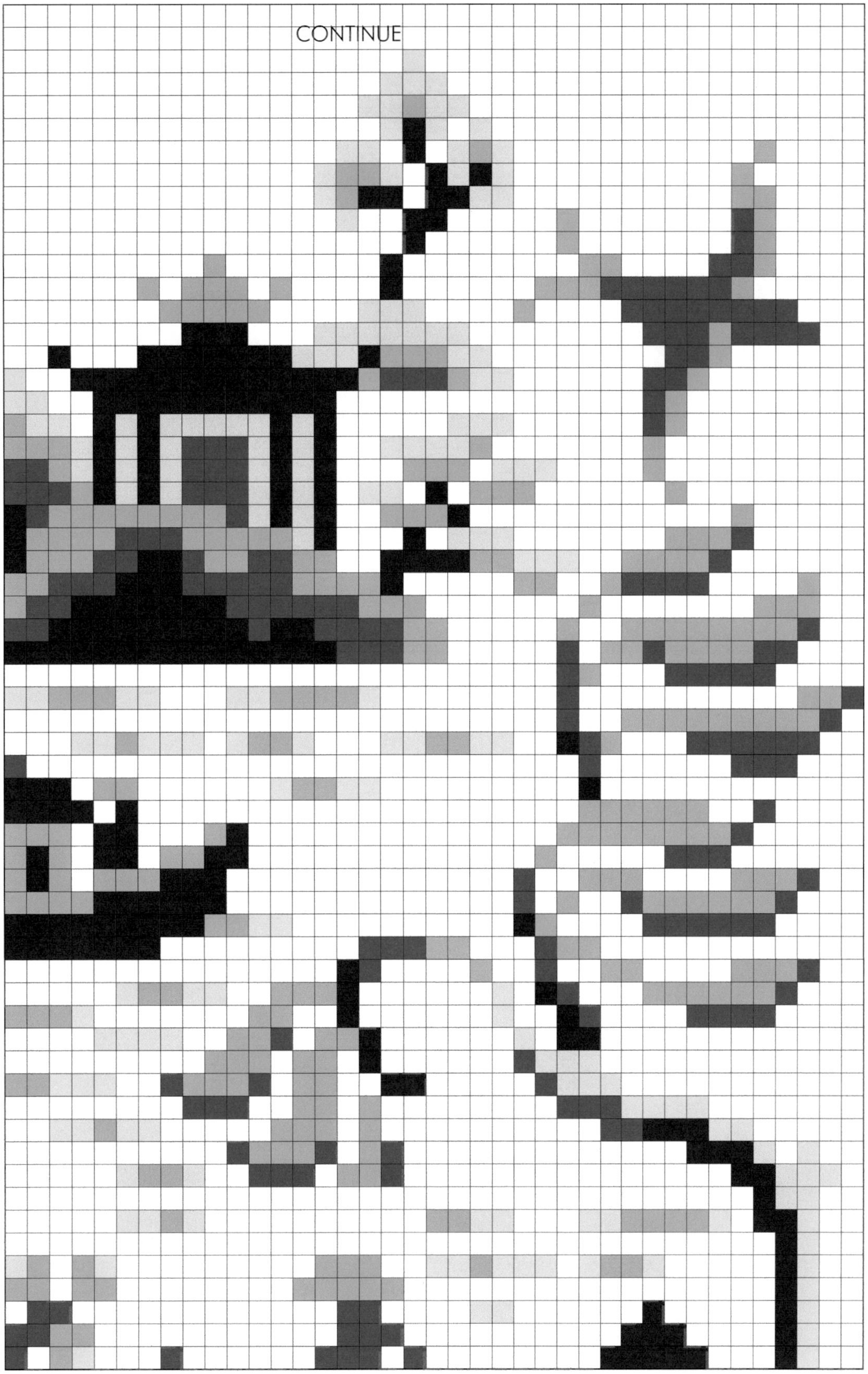

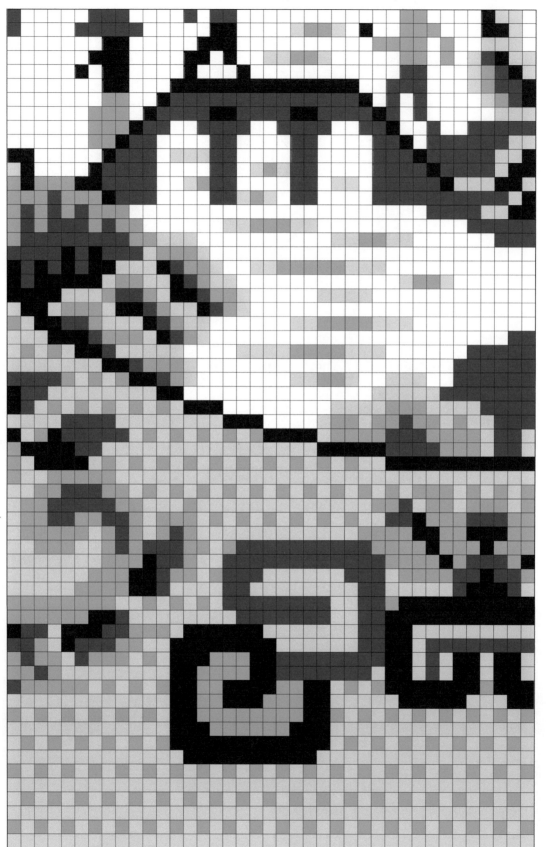

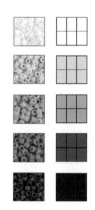

Repeating patterns

Inspired by quilting, bargello, and so much more. As shown in these examples, the patterns can be worked in multiple colors or in monochrome. They're wonderful for using up small amounts of leftover beads as bases for a focal decoration.

For each design on the following pages you'll find an overview of how the pattern works up when repeated, and an enlarged chart showing one repeat of the pattern. The color bar shows all the colors needed, but because there are limitless possibilities for color choice, Delica colors are not indicated. You know better than anyone what you have on hand.

Also given are the woven widths and the number of rows per repeat, so you can easily determine the number of repeats you will need.

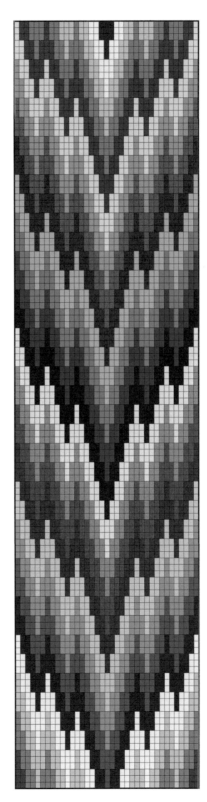
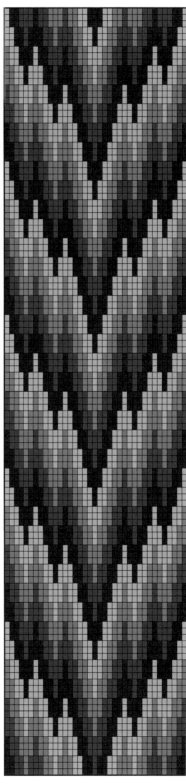

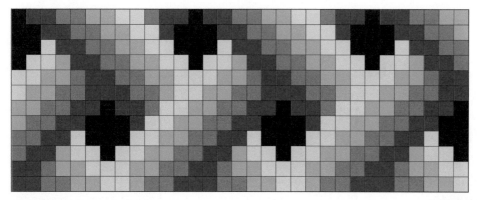

ONE FULL REPEAT

OVERVIEW

1

WIDTH/11-DELICAS	1.82"	4.6cm
WIDTH /15° SEED BEADS	1.55"	3.9cm
WIDTH /11° SEED BEADS	1.94"	4.7cm

WARP THREADS REQUIRED 32
REPEAT 31 WIDE x 12 ROWS

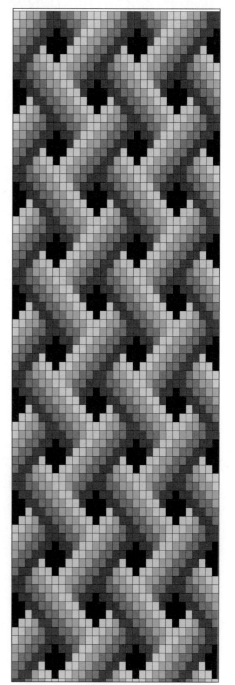

ONE FULL REPEAT

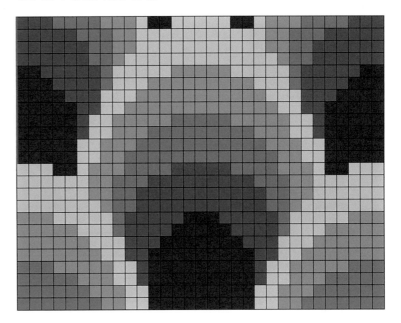

OVERVIEW

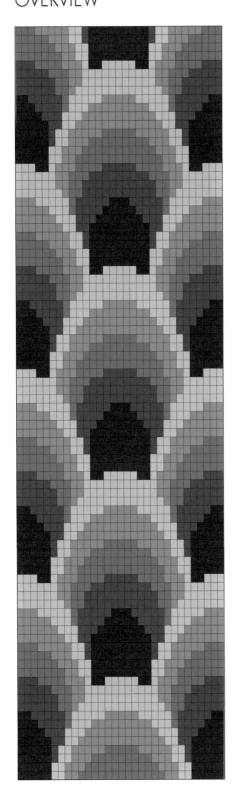

WIDTH/11-DELICAS	1.82"	4.6cm
WIDTH /15° SEED BEADS	1.55"	3.9cm
WIDTH /11° SEED BEADS	1.94"	4.7cm

2

WARP THREADS REQUIRED 32
REPEAT 31 WIDE x 24 ROWS

OVERVIEW

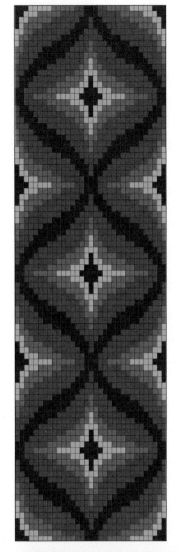

ONE FULL
REPEAT

4

WIDTH/11-DELICAS	2.1"	5.5cm
WIDTH /15° SEED BEADS	1.85"	4.7cm
WIDTH /11° SEED BEADS	2.3"	5.9cm

WARP THREADS REQUIRED 38
REPEAT 37 WIDE x 24 ROWS

3

WARP THREADS REQUIRED 34
REPEAT 33 WIDE x 30 ROWS

WIDTH/11-DELICAS	1.9"	4.9cm
WIDTH /15° SEED BEADS	1.65"	4.2cm
WIDTH /11° SEED BEADS	2.1"	5.2cm

ONE FULL
REPEAT

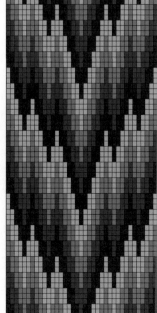

OVERVIEW

ONE FULL REPEAT

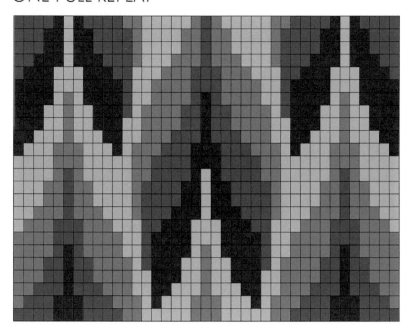

	A
	B
	C
	D

WIDTH/11-DELICAS	2.3"	5.8cm
WIDTH /15° SEED BEADS	1.95"	5cm
WIDTH /11° SEED BEADS	2.4"	6.2cm

WARP THREADS REQUIRED 40
REPEAT 39 WIDE x 24 ROWS

5

OVERVIEW

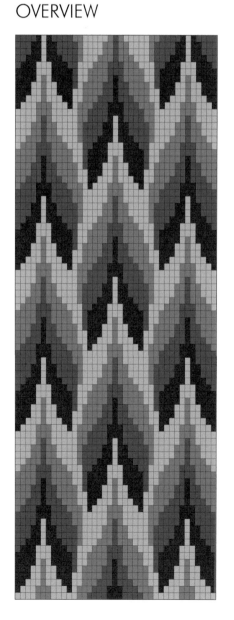

OVERVIEW

ONE FULL REPEAT

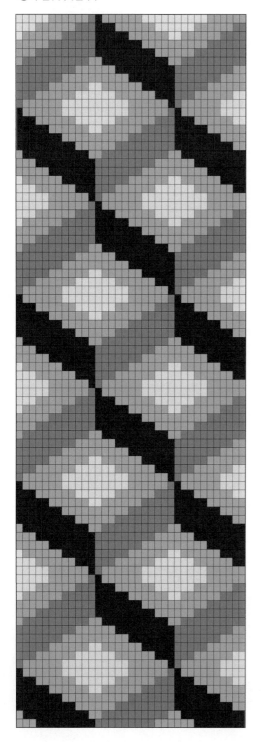

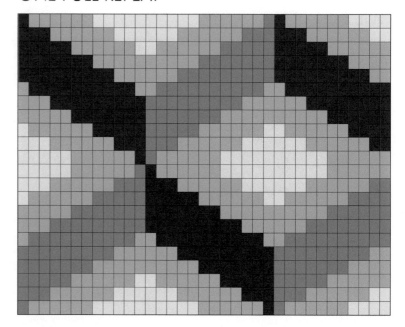

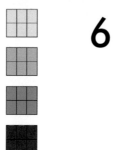

6

WIDTH/11-DELICAS	2"	5.3cm
WIDTH /15° SEED BEADS	1.75"	4.4cm
WIDTH /11° SEED BEADS	2.2"	5.6cm

WARP THREADS REQUIRED 36
REPEAT 35 WIDE x 24 ROWS

ONE FULL REPEAT

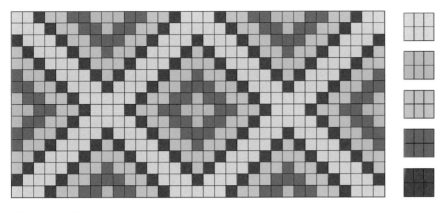

OVERVIEW

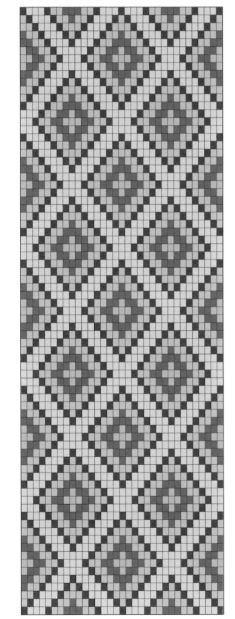

WIDTH/11-DELICAS	1.9"	4.9cm
WIDTH /15° SEED BEADS	1.65"	4.2cm
WIDTH /11° SEED BEADS	2.1"	5.2cm

WARP THREADS REQUIRED 34
REPEAT 33 WIDE x 16 ROWS

8

7

WARP THREADS REQUIRED 18
REPEAT 17 WIDE x 8 ROWS

WIDTH/11-DELICAS	1"	2.5cm
WIDTH /15° SEED BEADS	.85"	2.2cm
WIDTH /11° SEED BEADS	1.1"	2.7cm

ONE FULL REPEAT

OVERVIEW

ONE FULL REPEAT

OVERVIEW

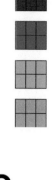

9

WARP THREADS REQUIRED 32
REPEAT 31 WIDE x 30 ROWS

WIDTH/11-DELICAS	1.82"	4.6cm
WIDTH /15° SEED BEADS	1.55"	3.9cm
WIDTH /11° SEED BEADS	1.94"	4.7cm

Finishing

Added closures (loop and bead/button, Clasps, magnetics) are added after the weave is removed from the loom. Buttonholes are added during the weave. The placement of buttons is figured in final sizing and is adjustable.

Loop and bead closure

In this simple closure the length of your woven piece only needs to be about 1/4" (6 mm) longer than the desired wrist size. Rondelles or disks are a great choice; in the example shown here, 6mm rondelles are secured to the second row in from the end with 15° seed beads on either side. Beads should be secured with a doubled thread, and you may need a fine needle such as a size 13 needle to make the second pass. Because you can shift the placement of the closure beads, there's a lot of adjustability with this method.

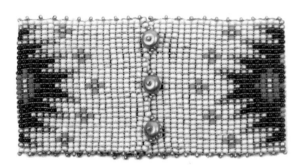

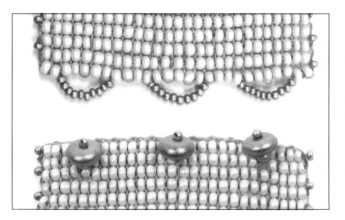

Loops should be sized to just barely fit over the bead; you may need some trial-and-error to get the correct fit. Loops are attached to the outermost row of the opposite end; if possible, reinforce this outer row with another pass of weft for strength. Loops need at least two passes of thread. This is an easy closure to operate and very comfortable to wear. Add the loops first, then align the beads to the loops for a neat closure.

This example of a loop and bead closure is worked on a fiber end. Adding a fiber end to your bead-woven design is a very effective way to incorporate an attractive closure.

Beaded button and buttonhole closure

Button/buttonhole closures can be woven right into the pattern at the start of the weave. In most cases the placement of the buttons can be adjusted to fine-tune sizing.

The basic idea in creating a buttonhole is to weave shortened sections adjacent to each other, thereby creating an open space between warp threads through which a button can be slipped. In "Serape" there are three buttonholes spaced evenly on one end of the bracelet, and three pearl "buttons" at the opposite end. Button placement is adjustable allowing for fine-tuning of the sizing of the bracelet.

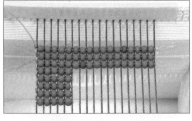

Shown at left is the start of a two-buttonhole closure. Three full rows are woven, then five shortened rows. Weave through the five shortened rows back to the three full rows, and bring the weft thread out in position to start another shortened section. There is no perfect way to weave through existing beads to add more sections; the red line in the photo at left shows an example of how it might be done. You'll likely need a fine needle (size 13) as thread will build up within the beads. Additional thread within bead holes will actually strengthen and secure the weave. When the three shortened sections are complete, weave two or more full rows to secure the sections together. You can place buttonholes within your pattern as well, as shown in the "Colors" chart.

In "Tribal" there are five buttonholes and buttons. You can see the progress of the construction in these three photos, where the first section is joined to the full rows, then the other sections. Note that both outer short sections are four beads wide and all four inner sections are six beads wide. This allows for even placement of the buttons across the width.

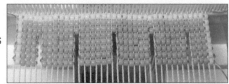

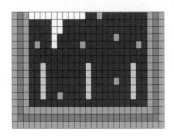

This portion of the "Colors" chart shows the placement of the buttonholes in yellow. You can mark your own charts for buttonhole placement and then incorporate the open areas into the weave.

106

Button and fiber buttonhole closure

Though designs included herein are intended for bead looming, you can easily incorporate fiber closures into your weaves. In "Paisley" both ends are worked in simple over-under weave, the most basic of the fiber weaving stitches. The buttonholes butt right up against the beaded weave. The buttons are literally sewn onto the fiber weave, which is in effect a little strip of fabric. As with buttons on a bead weave, the placement of the buttons on a fiber weave is adjustable for flexibility in sizing.

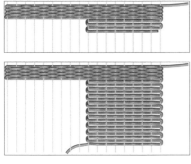

In these diagrams you can see one buttonhole woven into the very center of a fiber section. Note that the back and forth weave spans the same number of warps on either side of the buttonhole. The weave is tighty compressed as you progress to form a firm fabric.

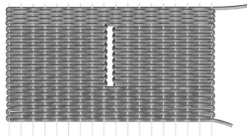

In this beaded necklace, the ends are woven in 10/2 perle cotton fiber and two buttonholes are place on one end, allowing the wearer to have a different shorter look as an option.

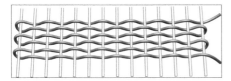 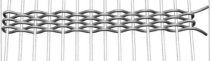 

In simple over-under weave, threads go over one warp thread then under the next. In the next row, threads are woven under one thread then over the next, alternating as shown at left. The weave is compressed as you go to form a dense, tight fabric. Starting and ending thread tails are woven into the underside of the weave as invisibly as possible; a sharp-pointed darning needle works well.

Fiber buttonholes are sectioned in the same manner as beaded button-holes, spaced harmoniously across the width. The three-hole closure shown below is secured together with a section of full rows.

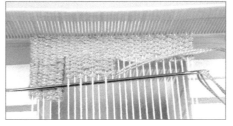 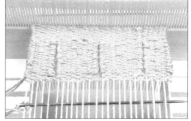

Beaded toggle closure

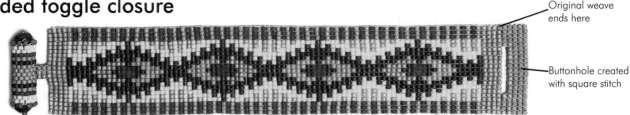

Original weave ends here

Buttonhole created with square stitch

This closure works best on a no-finish loom with cylinder beads, as there is considerable thread build-up in the opening end. You're creating a horizontal buttonhole for the toggle bar. Square stitch is used; it's a free-form version of the backstitch used in bead embroidery. Theoretically you could weave any charted design in square stitch, but it does take time. If you decide in advance that you're going to use this closure, leave long beading nylon thread tails (24" +) at the end of the loom, and then use them in adding the square stitch.

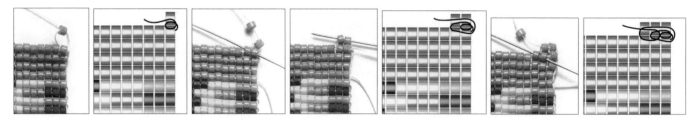

Starting on either side of the beaded strip, pick up one bead and form a loop by running outward through the bead on the end row. Run inward through the added bead, and take out the slack. Pick up another bead and run outward through the second bead on the outermost weave row. Bring the thread out of the outermost bead and take out the slack. Run inward through the two added beads. Pick up another bead and run outward through the third and second beads on the outermost weave row. Run the thread inward through the third and second added beads. Take out the slack.

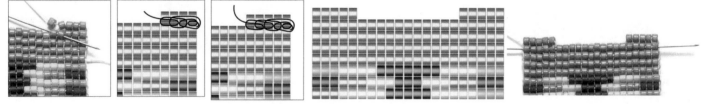

Continue in this manner, looping beads in place with inward and outward passes of thread until there are five beads added to the weave row. As each bead is added, take the slack out of the thread so the beads align neatly on top of the outermost loom-woven row. Run through the outermost weave row, and bring the thread out between the fourth and fifth beads (red dot). Recreate this five-bead motif at the opposite side of the outermost row. When that motif is complete, run through the entire outermost weave row and bring the thread out on the starting side.

Add a second group of five beads over the original five.
Pick up twelve beads. Run inward through the innermost bead of the left motif. Loop the last bead added to the innermost bead of the added five beads. The span of eleven beads should align with the eleven bead section of the outermost loomed row. Take the slack out of the thread but don't pull too tightly or the buttonhole may pucker.

Continue as before and complete the row to the end. Thereafter, add three complete rows of beads, using the eleven beads of the span as part of the base for these rows. When the rows are complete, weave back and forth through the rows to reinforce and strengthen the buttonhole. Secure and trim the thread. The horizontal buttonhole is now complete.

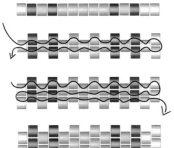

To create the peyote stitch toggle bar, start with the beads of the first two rows. Add the beads of the third row (the initial threading of beads creates the first TWO rows), then continue adding rows back and forth until there are ten edge beads as shown in the diagram. Add one row of yellow beads in brick stitch, as detailed in the diagram. Work across the full row until the peyote strip is symmetrical. This completes the weaving of the toggle strip.

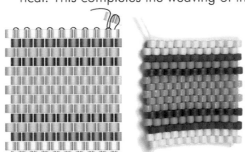

Roll the peyote strip into a tube and "zip" the edges together to create a hollow tube. If your tube collapses, you can roll paper and insert it into the opening, but be sure to keep a thread path open in the center. **Decorate the ends of the zipped tube;** I used one 15° over each pair of edge beads, and 6mm rondelles anchored with the same 15°. This is optional but will improve the appearance of the toggle bar.

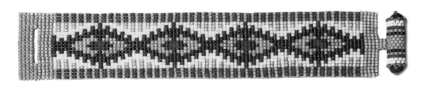

Fold-over ends

Fold-over ends start out open and are folded over the end of the loomed piece. These are sometimes called "ribbon ends" but there is a difference, in that ribbon ends generally have claws to grip the fabric. Claws are not the best idea on crushable glass beads. To use a ribbon end, weave to the depth of the ribbon end in fiber on both ends of the woven piece, so the claws will just cover the fiber area and not the beads.

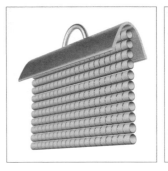

First GENEROUSLY glue the end of the weave, spread glue on the inside of the fold-over and then use small pliers GENTLY to fold the end until it fits neatly but not so tightly that it damages the beads. Once the end is in place, wipe away any excess glue and then attach the clasp of your choice; lobster claw, toggle, chains, anything that can be attached to the loop on the fold-over. Often, chains are attached to the fold-over loop to create sublime adjustability, and this is a good practice if you're making a piece to be sold, and can't predetermine the wrist size of the buyer.

Slide ends

Similar in concept to fold-overs but pre-shaped to fit over the end of the weave. As with fold-overs you can attach any style of clasp to the loop, offering lots of adjustability in sizing. Slide the tube opening over the last row of beads. A thin swipe of glue on the ends of the beads will keep the slide in position.

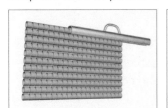

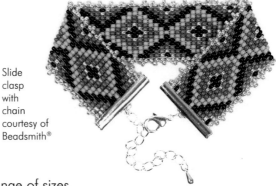

Slide clasp with chain courtesy of Beadsmith®

Magnetic clasps

Magnetic clasps come in a good range of sizes and shapes, and can be adapted to the size of your weave with a few tricks. In this example you can see the three rows of 11° seed beads woven at both ends of the loomed piece; these will be unseen within the clasp. The number of rows depends on the depth of the clasp opening. The critical measurements on your clasp are the INSIDE DIMENSIONS. In this case, the weave is 1 5/8" (about 40 mm) so the inside opening needs to be slightly longer. The width of the inside opening is 3mm, which will fit both 11°s and size 11 cylinders. I padded the three end rows with a piece of non-woven cut the same size to ensure a good fit. I smeared glue on the inside walls of the clasp AND along the edge of the outermost woven row of beads. Using a toothpick will enable you to push the weave fully into the clasp opening and create an attractive end.

When more thickness is needed to make the weave fit snugly into the clasp opening, you can weave a few extra rows and create a "hem" that is secured with a few stitches. With a no-finish loom, prepare for this in advance and size accordingly. Make sure the hems are folded into the same side on both ends. Use a thick smear of glue on the outer edge of the hem before inserting the end into the opening. A toothpick will enable you to push the hemmed end fully into the opening.

The magnetic clasp on "Poncho" is decorated with a glued-on front layer of a polymer clay design. The thin sheet (1.5mm) of clay was baked separately from the clasp, since magnetics can be weakened by heat over 175° F (129°C). While the glue was drying, a book was placed over the assembly to insure good contact. When the glue was thoroughly dry, the edges of the clay were trimmed with a sharp knife to precisely fit the top of the clasp. A coating of Modge Podge was added for a glossy effect.

Adding a safety strap to the finishing on a magnetic clasp is good practice, since magnets would much rather live on refrigerators and gas pumps than on your wrist. The example at right shows a crocheted bracelet using the recommended technique. A simple short strand of seed beads, just long enough so the piece will fit over your wrist, will work well and can be tucked under when worn. Make a double pass of thread through the strap. Safety straps cannot be used on necklaces, but there's less need for them.

Just a clasp

Sometimes you just want to sew a clasp on the end of the piece. There are some gorgeous clasps that can really enhance both the look and the functionality of your looming. In the leather and bead example at right, the long slide clasp is attached through the loops with 15° seed beads; the weave beads 11°s. This bracelet has an Ultrasuede backing, which allows you to pass right through the weave without going through the woven beads themselves; if you are weaving with beads alone, you may want to go through the hole in a bead

rather than just the warp threads. You'll need a bead sized to both fit through the loop on your clasp and accept two passes of your thread. You can switch to a finer thread, and use a size 13 needle to make this process work smoothly. Before you begin make sure the attachment beads will fit through the loops of your clasp.

Care and feeding

In general, **beads can be cleaned in water**, as long as you don't rub them. If you have any doubt about the durability of your bead's finish, contact the manufacturer for guidelines. In most cases, as long as the water is **not too hot**, it's safe to dip beads in warm soapy water. To rinse, dip the beads in clean lukewarm water, **don't spray beads with water**, as finishes can be damaged by that kind of water pressure. You can **gently pat the beads dry** after washing, then lay your weave out flat to dry, shaped to size if needed.

Cosmetics can be damaging to beads and their finishes. Avoid oily skin creams or perfumes in the areas where the beads will contact your skin.

Nylon and polyester threads will not be damaged by water; most marine upholstery threads are nylon or polyester.

Cotton and silk threads may shrink when wet but can be reshaped in original size to dry. **Tencel or rayon threads WILL shrink** significantly and should be avoided as warp. They can be restored to original size when dry but it's a process! Allow washed woven pieces to completely air-dry.

If you are attaching a clasp or closure with thread, it's good practice to **replace the attachment threading from time to time**, as threads may weaken when exposed to friction and movement.

Index

What's next?
Try combining
beads and fibers

About the author

Ann Benson is an internationally acclaimed designer of beading, needlearts, and weaving, active for over fifty years in the crafting world. She is a renowned expert on all forms of bead crochet and bead embroidery, and is recognized for the accuracy and clarity of her directions and tutorials. She maintains a YouTube library of dozens of video tutorials and on-line classes, and a catalog of downloadable print tutorials on annbensonbeading.com.

She is the mother of two fabulous grown women and the grandmother of seven delightful children. She lives in Port Orange, Florida in winter, and on Cape Cod in summer, with her husband retired police detective Gary Frost.

I welcome your polite comments and criticisms and eagerly seek corrections! Please contact me via annbensonbeading.com with suggestions, errata, and other concerns.

Please feel free to review any of my beading books and novels on your purchase platform such as Amazon, Etsy, Barnes & Noble, and Kobo, or any other place where my books are sold.

Permissions

Items made from the designs in this work may be sold as finished products; design attribution is requested. Patterns from this work are for personal use ONLY and may not be sold, either in whole or part. Teachers wishing to use materials from this work should first contact the author via annbensonbeading.com and may be given permission to use materials for teaching purposes with attribution.

Resources

On annbensonbeading.com, you will find:

- Sourcing for seed beads, threads, and tools
- Links to on-line video tutorials
- Color cards for Miyuki, Toho, Matsuno, Preciosa, Jablonex seed beads
- Printable tutorials

Beading books by Ann Benson

Encyclopedia of Tubular Bead Crochet (print, digital, Kindle)
Dimensional Bead Crochet (digital)
Tapestry Bead Crochet (print with DVD)
Beautiful Bead Stitching on Canvas (print)
Designer Beading Bead Crochet (print with DVD)
Beadwork Basics (print)
Bead Weaving (print)

Novels by Ann Benson
The Plague Trilogy:
(The Plague Tales, The Burning Road, The Physician's Tale)

Stand-alone novels:
Thief of Souls, Ambrosia

Made in United States
Troutdale, OR
10/16/2024

23804477R00069